GREEN POLITICAL THOUGHT

GREEN POLITICAL THOUGHT

An Introduction

Andrew Dobson

London
UNWIN HYMAN
Boston   Sydney   Wellington

Published by the Academic Division of
Unwin Hyman Ltd
15/17 Broadwick Street, London W1V 1FP, UK

Unwin Hyman Inc.,
8 Winchester Place, Winchester, Mass. 01890, USA

Allen & Unwin (Australia) Ltd,
8 Napier Street, North Sydney, NSW 2060, Australia

Allen & Unwin (New Zealand) Ltd in association with the
Port Nicholson Press Ltd,
Compusales Building, 75 Ghuznee Street, Wellington 1, New Zealand

First published in 1990

British Library Cataloguing in Publication Data

Dobson, Andrew
    Green political thought: an introduction.
    1. Ecology. Political aspects
    I. Title
    304.2
    ISBN 0-04-445244-6
    ISBN 0-04-445245-4 (Pbk)

Library of Congress Cataloging in Publication Data

Available on request

Typeset in 10½/13 point Bembo by Fotographics (Bedford) Ltd
and printed in Great Britain by Billing & Sons, London and Worcester

Contents

For Concha Pérez Moreno

Acknowledgements

This book began life as a Workers' Educational Association course on Green politics in Oxford in 1986–7, and the learning process which I began there has continued in the presence of two successive groups of students studying post-industrial politics at Keele University. I owe a debt of gratitude to all those who attended these courses for their enthusiasm and for their commitment to the difficult business of coaxing some coherence out of my confusion.

I have benefited enormously from conversations with David Hay, Anna Bramwell, David Pepper, Jon Carpenter, Jean Lambert, Tim Andrewes, and Andrew Simms, while Tim O'Riordan and Warwick Fox have given me valuable guidance in correspondence. Similarly, various anonymous publishers' referees pointed out weak spots as the project unfolded and I have done my best to act on their wise advice. In this context my editor, Gordon Smith, has been a very gratifying source of good sense and timely encouragement throughout. Thanks are also due to my brother, Mike Dobson, who not only supplied a stream of scientific articles on the state of the environment, but whose work for the Río Mazan project in a cloud forest in Ecuador provided me with a salutary visit to the frontline. At the same time I could not have done without the invaluable secretarial assistance which Pauline Weston and Ruth Battye have unhesitatingly lent me.

But my deepest debt of gratitude is owed to my colleague Margaret Canovan for responding to frequent requests for help with a forbearance and a readiness far beyond that which I could reasonably have expected. She was quick to spot mistakes and generous with suggestions, and I have benefited

greatly from her interventions. Needless to say, no-one but
myself can accept responsibility for any shortcomings which
may remain.

Andrew Dobson
Keele University
October 1989

Introduction

In 1988 *Time* magazine broke its tradition, for only the second time in its history, of providing us with a Man of the Year (it usually *is* a man) and placed a planet on the front cover instead – the planet Earth. Robert Miller, the publisher, wrote that this decision 'had its origin in the scorching summer of 1988, when environmental disasters – droughts, floods, forest fires, polluted beaches – dominated the news' (2 January 1989, p. 10). Indeed all around the world in 1988 and 1989 environmental interpretations of 'natural' calamities seemed to many more people than ever before to begin to make sense, from floods in Bangladesh and landslides in Bolivia to avalanches in Austria and starvation in the Sudan. The ozone layer has become a source of popular preoccupation and people ponder unusually mild winters (in Britain at least), wondering whether the long-promised 'greenhouse effect' is not already with us. Cuddly, furry animals like the panda have long been a source of conservationist sympathy, but an extension of appreciation seemed to take place towards the end of 1988 when three gashed and barnacled whales trapped beneath the Arctic ice riveted television's attention and prompted the combined efforts of the world's most powerful navies to save them.

In Britain the membership of environmental organizations is rising spectacularly – in 1988 Friends of the Earth alone gained 15,000 new members, an increase of 30 per cent, while in the aftermath of the 1989 European elections the Green Party was receiving 250 membership applications per day. Although this might be no more than a temporary phenomenon, rather like the transient swelling of the Campaign for Nuclear Disarmament in the early 1960s and the early to mid-1980s, it seems unlikely that the analyses that have given rise to such a flurry of activity and concern will so easily be marginalized, or that the dangers that prompted them will so conveniently be made to 'go away'. At the same time, some powerful and seemingly unlikely individuals have apparently climbed aboard the environmental bandwagon. The British Prime Minister Margaret Thatcher used to include environmentalists as part of the 'enemy within' – unpatriotically gnawing away, like the miners and other agitators, at the sickening heart of British society. So it is hardly surprising that even her closest advisers were said to be startled at the content of her speech to the Royal Society in September 1988 in which she said what the enemy within had been saying all along: that we may unwittingly be performing an experiment on the planet, the outcome of which we cannot predict with certainty.

The Conservative Party, like the other major political parties and along with the countless individuals, groups and organizations who are discovering the environment as a political issue towards the end of the twentieth century, now publicly considers itself as steward, rather than master, of the planet we inhabit. A high-profile Green Consumer Week during 12–18 September 1988, in which we were urged to 'shop for a better environment' by buying the right things, was followed by a flurry of international conferences on the ozone layer and the 'greenhouse effect' in 1989. Then the Green Party's spectacular showings in the May European elections, together with an increased Green presence in the European parliament, seemed finally to confirm that Green politics is now on the political agenda.

But is it? To answer in the affirmative is clearly to beg the question: what is Green politics? All the positions mentioned so far are informed by a concern for the environment and there is an overriding sense in which this is held to be sufficient to call them Green positions. A closer look, however, suggests that this is not the case, because the differences of intention between the various people and groups who show a concern for the environment are often greater than the similarities.

Organizations such as the National Trust in Britain, for example, can sensibly be said to be concerned for the environment, and that concern is expressed principally through the restoration of and care for old and striking buildings and their grounds. Greenpeace, too, is clearly concerned for the environment, but it adopts a very different approach to that of the National Trust. Greenpeace, and other organizations like it such as Friends of the Earth, typically confront the negative effects on the environment of late-twentieth century society, and try to ameliorate them. They will do this either through concentrating on spectacular forms of direct action, as in the case of Greenpeace, or through patient and expert lobbying, the preferred tactic of Friends of the Earth. For the sake of clarity we can refer to organizations such as the National Trust as *conservation* organizations, and to organizations such as Greenpeace or Friends of the Earth as *environmental* organizations. I must make it clear at the outset that the present book is about neither of these; it directly concerns neither conservationism nor environmentalism, although it turns out (for reasons that will become clear) that something has to be said from time to time about the latter. Nor is this a book about the politics of Green parties, as such, for the content of this politics is easily available in Green manifestos. The relationship between ecologism (the subject of this book) and Green parties is of the same kind as that between, say, socialism and social democratic parties.

What this book is about is Green politics, inasmuch as a Green concern for the environment leads not (only) to the care of country houses or the saving of the whale, but to the desire to restructure the whole of political, social and economic life. Neither conservationists nor environmentalists believe that the Good Life is much different from the one we presently lead, but political ecologists most certainly do. It is in this sense that ecologism can properly take its place alongside other political ideologies; in common with other political ideologies it has things to say across the whole range of political, social and economic life. Ecologism cannot be seen as simply embedded in other political ideologies – it is a political ideology in its own right, and this book sketches its content. My suggestion is that if we confuse Green politics (capital 'G') with either conservationism or environmentalism (the latter being green with a small 'g') then we severely distort and misunderstand the nature of the Green challenge to the political, social, economic and scientific consensus that dominates the late twentieth century. We are, indeed, in danger of losing sight of the fact that it is a challenge at all. I shall say something more about this shortly.

First, though, this has both 'academic' and 'practical' ramifications. In the context of the intellectual attempt to make sense of our social and political environment, it would be a matter of serious self-deception to misread Green politics and substitute what the newspapers tell us it is for what it 'really' is. We are led to believe that Green politics concerns lead-free petrol, organic vegetables and environmentally sound aerosols. It does, of course, but these issues do not exhaust the content of Green politics and any systematic account of the Green political phenomenon has to begin from that understanding. The Queen of England does not suddenly become a political ecologist by virtue of having her fleet of limousines converted to lead-free petrol.

The 'practical' outcome of such an understanding might be to lead us to question the viability of environmentalist solutions to ecological problems – this is certainly what political ecologists will want us to do. Let us assume, for example, that there is a consensus over the issue of global warming: that the build-up of greenhouse gases in the atmosphere will lead to an average rise in temperature that is likely to have disruptive effects across the planet over the next several decades. From that premise one can derive various possible courses of action. We could fit carbon dioxide scrubbers to industrial chimneys, ban chlorofluorocarbons in aerosols, and we could equip our cars with catalytic convertors. But we could also de-industrialize, and ban cars and aerosols altogether. Somewhere in between we could seek to shift the terms of debate such that the onus of justification was placed on those who want to continue to produce cars and aerosols, rather than on those who call them into question.

In the context of this spectrum there is a growing tendency to believe that Green politics is its 'reformist' wing. Yet Green radicalism and green reformism are not only analytically different in terms of the *amount* of change they prescribe, but also qualitatively different in terms of the *kind* of change they prescribe, and so I take the unusual step in this book of claiming that what is now normally held to be Green politics is not Green at all, but green, or even 'green'. My object of study is what I take to be Green (with a capital 'G') politics, and the intention is to keep its radical nature in view at all times. Only this will allow us to see ecologism as a political ideology in its own right.

Such a strategy will also help us to understand the apparently heretical suggestion that the West German Green Party is not a party of ecology in the sense in which I think we ought to understand the word. We are confronted with the irony that the most well-known political–institutional expression of Green politics is not really Green at all because 'a Green philosophy, as a foundation for a purely ecological policy, was no longer seen as adequate, although writings in this vein . . . were very popular in the early stages of the movement' (Hülsberg, 1988, p. 133). I shall argue that the less visible but more fundamental manifestations of the Green movement are greener than the West German Green Party – at least from the perspective of the centre of gravity I am going to develop in this book.

This connects back to an earlier suggestion: that to mis-understand the nature of Green politics is to misconceive its historical significance as a challenge to the political, social and scientific consensus that has dominated the last two or three hundred years of public life. Green politics self-consciously confronts dominant paradigms, and my task here is to ensure that it is not swallowed up by them and the interests they often seem to serve. In this sense it is in a similar position to notions like post-industrialism. Michael Marien is right to suggest that, contrary to general opinion, there is not one but 'two visions of post-industrial society' and, importantly, that one of these is dominant and the other is subordinate. If we allow the subordinate one to disappear we risk intellectual sloppiness and

[5]

are likely to mistake consensus for disagreement, and the same goes for green and Green politics – or what I have called environmentalism and ecologism.

Marien writes that there are 'two completely different modes of usage: "post-industrial society" as a technological, affluent, service society, and "post-industrial society" as a decentralised agrarian economy following in the wake of a failed industrialism' (1977, p. 416), and suggests that the former is dominant with respect to the latter. Clearly the second usage constitutes a challenge to the first usage in that it calls itself by the same name while reconstituting its meaning. Using his typology, Marien sensitizes us to the variety of possible interpretations of post-industrial society. This variety would be invisible if we were to pay attention only to the dominant interpretation: that of an affluent, service economy.

Analogously, I have suggested that dominant and subordinate understandings of Green politics are beginning to emerge from the welter of interest that presently surrounds the topic. The point is to remain open to the existence of these understandings rather than to let the bright light of the dominant one obscure the subordinate one behind.

But of course it is not simply a question of analogy. It just happens that Marien's dominant version of post-industrialism – a technological, affluent, service society – is a fair description of the late-twentieth-century political aspiration to which most people would probably subscribe, if asked. We are certainly encouraged at every turn to aspire to it, at any rate. Now the content of post-industrialism in this dominant sense can work powerful magic on all with which it comes into contact – it moulds challenges to it in its own image and so draws their sting. This is, I think, precisely what has happened to environmental politics as it has emerged from the wings on to the main stage. There is now a perfectly respectable (but erroneous) claim to be made that Green politics can be a part of a technological, affluent, service society – a part, in other words, of Marien's dominant version of what post-industrial society both is, and might be, like. This is the green politics of carbon dioxide scrubbers on industrial chimneys, CFC-free aerosols and car exhausts fitted with catalytic convertors.

In this guise, green politics presents no sort of a challenge at all to the late-twentieth-century consensus over the desirability of affluent, technological, service societies. But my understanding of the historical significance of Green politics is that it constitutes precisely such a challenge, and that we shall lose sight of that significance if we conceive of it only in its reformist mode – a mode that reinforces affluence and technology rather than calling them into question. Green politics is far more a friend of the subordinate interpretation of post-industrialism – a decentralized economy following in the wake of a failed industrialism – than of its dominant counterpart. Jonathon Porritt and Nicholas Winner assert that,

> the most radical [Green aim] seeks nothing less than a non-violent revolution to overthrow our whole polluting, plundering and materialistic industrial society and, in its place, to create a new economic and social order which will allow human beings to live in harmony with the planet. In those terms, the Green Movement lays claim to being the most radical and important political and cultural force since the birth of socialism. (1988, p. 9)

It is in these terms that I see Green politics in this book, first, so as to keep a fuller picture of the movement in mind than is presently the case; second, to understand better the challenge that it presents to the dominant consensus; and third, to establish ecologism as a political ideology in its own right. This last is important because I believe Barbara Goodwin (among others) to be wrong in calling ecologism a 'cross-cutting ideology' which 'falls into other existing ideological categories' (1987, p. vii).

In a sense Porritt and Winner do the movement a disfavour by likening the profundity of its challenge to that of early socialism. Much of socialism's intellectual work, at least, had already been done by the time it came on the scene. Liberal theorists had long since laid the ground for calls for liberty and equality, and socialism's job was to pick up and reconstitute the pieces created by liberalism's apparent failure to turn theory into practice.

In this sense the Green movement is in a position more akin to that of the early liberals than that of the early socialists – it is self-consciously seeking to call into question an entire world view rather than tinker with one that already exists. For the sake of convenience, but at the risk of blind blundering on territory where specialists themselves quite properly fear to tread, the world view that modern political ecologists challenge is the one that grew out of the (early) Enlightenment. Norman Hampson has suggested a number of characteristics salient to the Enlightenment world view: 'a period when the culture of the educated man was thought to take in the whole of educated knowledge' (1979, p. 11); 'that man was to a great extent the master of his own destiny' (ibid., p. 35); that 'God was a mathematician whose calculations, although infinite in their subtle complexity, were accessible to man's intelligence' (ibid., pp. 37–8); and that 'universal reason' was held to be preferable to 'local habit', principally because it helps to drive out superstitition (ibid., p. 152).

The general tenor of these characteristics is the exaltation of human beings and their particular faculties (e.g. reason) – the placing of the human being in a pre-eminent position with respect to the rest of, not only terrestrial phenomena, but the universe at large. If Isaac Newton humbly saw himself as a boy playing on the sea shore finding only the odd shiny pebble while the 'great ocean of truth' lay before him, this was surely more because he hadn't the time to set sail than because he thought he lacked the equipment to do so. This belief in the centrality of 'man' was encapsulated in the principle of *bienfaisance*, or benevolence, according to which the world was the best of all possible worlds for human beings. Hampson quotes Pluche as writing that 'It is for him [Man] that the sun rises; it is for him that the stars shine', and goes on to observe that, 'Almost everything could be pressed into service, from the density of water, which Fenelon considered exactly calculated to facilitate navigation, to the shape of the water-melon, which makes it easy to slice' (ibid., p. 81). In these respects the Enlightenment attitude was that the world had been made for human beings and that, in principle, nothing in it could be kept secret from them.

In a tortuous way this attitude has remained dominant ever since in the cultures and societies that have most obviously incubated the modern Green movement. They inform, too, Marien's dominant interpretation of what post-industrial society both is and ought to be: Baconian science has helped produce its technology and its material affluence, and the Promethean project to which the Enlightenment gave birth in its modern form is substantially intact. Now the historical significance of Green politics as I see it is that it constitutes a challenge to this project and to the norms and practices that sustain it. Green politics explicitly seeks to decentre the human being, to question mechanistic science and its technological consequences, to refuse to believe that the world was made for human beings – and it does this because it has been led to wonder whether dominant post-industrialism's project of material affluence is either desirable or sustainable. All this will be missed if we choose to restrict our understanding of Green politics to what is becoming its principal guise: an environmentalism that seeks a cleaner service economy, sustained by cleaner technology and producing cleaner affluence.

These thoughts on the Enlightenment help to identify ecologism's present historical significance, but there is danger here too. The analytic temptation is to see the ideology as a re-creation of the romantic reaction that the Enlightenment and then early forms of industrialization themselves brought about. So we cast ecologism in terms of passion opposing reason, of the joys of a bucolic life and of mystery as against transparency. And of course it is true that most manifestations of the Green movement argue for a repopulation of the countryside and for the reawakening of a sense of awe in the face of natural phenomena.

At the same time, however, modern Green politics turns out to be based on a self-consciously hard-headed assessment of the unsustainability of present political and economic practices – it is remarkable, indeed, to see the extent to which the success of modern political ecology has been mediated and sustained by scientific research. This could hardly be said of the romantic reaction to the Enlightenment. Similarly, ecologism's political Utopia is (by and large) informed by interpretations of the principle of equality – a principle that was minted and put into circulation during the Enlightenment, and certainly not popular with romantics. Again, as far as romanticism is concerned, Green politics has little time for individualism or for geniuses, and one suspects (although this will be disputed by members of the movement) that the nonconformity so beloved of romantics would be a pretty scarce commodity in Green communities. Finally, if we hold the Green movement to believe that one can only recognize the value of the natural world through intuition (as we are likely to do if we see it merely as a resurgence of romanticism), then we are blind to the enormous range and influence of rationalist attempts to account for such value, and which are of great importance to the movement's intellectual archaeology.

So while (in terms of its present historical significance) Green politics ought to be characterized as a challenge to the contemporary consensus over norms and practices that has its most immediate sources in the early Enlightenment, it would be a mistake to think it pays no mind whatever to those norms and practices. And this would be an especially big mistake if we were to jump to the conclusion that modern Green politics is only a form of reincarnated romanticism. To guard against this we should say that its challenge most generally takes the form of an attempt to shift the terms of the burden of persuasion from those who would question the dominant post-industrial embodiment (an affluent, technological, service society) of politics and society, onto those who would defend it. In doing so Greens may sometimes speak, even if often *sotto voce*, in the Enlightenment idiom.

[10]

My reasons for talking about Green politics in a specific way in this book are therefore primarily analytical, but there is also a literary–strategic reason. Implicit in what has been said so far is the idea that, just as there are many socialisms and many liberalisms, so there are many ecologisms. Writers on ideologies are consistently confronted with the challenge of defining the apparently indefinable, in the sense that the historical and therefore changing nature of their subject makes simple elucidation very difficult. The problem is compounded by the plethora of individuals, movements and parties that have called themselves (for example) 'liberal' or 'socialist'. On the face of it, the differences between the bearers of these claims are often greater than their similarities.

There are essentially two strategies available to would-be writers on ideologies in the face of this difficulty. The first is simply to take on board the multiplicity of 'definitions' and to make it the organizing principle of the study. Thus the history of the ideology and the people and movements that have carried it are present throughout, and the plurality of meanings of, say, socialism, is preserved. An advantage of this method is that it provides no hasty answer to the original begged question: 'what is socialism'?, and if the method is followed wisely it can also be used explicitly to stress the essential historicity of ideologies. This is an important point to make in its own right.

The disadvantage, however, is that such books on ideologies are very awkward to read. There is a sense in which the landscape of such a study is too flat to provide for points of reference; the reader is so preoccupied with peering into the distance, looking for landmarks, that the ground beneath passes virtually unnoticed.

In the light of this, an alternative strategy would be to provide a series of landmarks at the outset. This involves making an explicit pitch for a specific understanding of the ideology in question, around which the rest of the discussion can revolve. This does of course provide an answer to the begged question referred to above, but it need do so only temporarily. The employment of this strategy requires an open recognition of the provisional nature of the original understanding, and involves an invitation to refer throughout to alternative senses of the ideology in question. This is the strategy I have chosen to follow in this book, and this introduction and the next chapter provide the necessary landmarks.

Finally, a remark needs to be made about the use of the word 'ideology' here. The study of ideology is immensely more complex than the standard 'functional' definition of the word would have us believe. At a more profound level than this, ideology 'asks about the bases and validity of our most fundamental ideas' (McLellan, 1986, p. 1) and as such involves us in critical thought about the most hidden presuppositions of present social and political life – even more hidden than those that political ecologists claim to have uncovered. Drawing on Marx, this conception of ideology urges us to take nothing for granted and suggests that words used in any given description of the world are opaque rather than translucent, and demand deciphering.

However, it seems that there is still something useful to be said about socialism, liberalism and conservatism from within the functional idiom, if only in the sense that we can indeed sensibly view political ideologies as providing 'the concepts, categories, images and ideas by means of which people make sense of their social and political world, form projects, come to a certain consciousness of their place in that world and act in it' (Donald and Hall, 1986, p. x). It is this functional understanding of ideology that informs the content of the present book. I aim to set out the ideas with which the Green movement *describes* the political and social world, *prescribes* action within it, and seeks to *motivate* us to such action. This is an uncontroversial perspective in the context of describing political ideologies, but the understanding of 'ideology' that it presupposes is far from uncontroversial in the wider context of the study of ideology itself. In this wider context, both ecologism and the present book about it would have to be subjected to interrogation.

CHAPTER 1

Thinking about ecologism

Having written the last two general election manifestos for the Ecology Party, I would be hard put even now to say what our ideology is. (Porritt, 1986, p. 9)

The first and most important point to be made about ecologism is that it is not the same as environmentalism. As Jonathon Porritt, currently director of Friends of the Earth and the leading speaker for the Green movement in Britain, has written: 'It seems quite clear that whereas a concern for the environment is an essential part of being green, it is, as we shall see, by no means the same thing as being green' (1986, p. 5). The principal difference between the two is that ecologism argues that care for the environment (a fundamental characteristic of the ideology in its own right, of course) presupposes radical changes in our relationship with it, and thus in our mode of social and political life. Environmentalism, on the other hand, would argue for a 'managerial' approach to environmental problems, secure in the belief that they can be solved without fundamental changes in present values or patterns of production and consumption.

Much more will be said about this in later chapters, but it is important to accept this distinction early on: as I suggested in the Introduction, ecologism has a developed sense of the Good Life that is different in important and fundamental respects from that of other political ideologies. Environmentalism, however, could be a sub-plot (although likely to be embedded rather uneasily) in a main story such as liberalism or socialism.

[13]

Attempts to view ecologism in the same light seriously underestimate its status, and are often based on confusing it with environmentalism.

This maps rather neatly onto the time-honoured distinction between political parties and pressure groups: the latter are generally held to be single-issue organizations, while the former are expected to have points of view across the whole gamut of political and social life. In this context, campaigns to save the whale or stop the fur trade are not Green in the full sense I want to give the word, and even organizations like Greenpeace and Friends of the Earth (which campaign on many fronts at the same time) stop short of being wholly Green. This is because, while many of their members might individually subscribe to the necessity for the radical changes in our political and social life referred to above, the organizations do not explicitly do so. I should warn at the same time against a too-hasty identification of Green parties with ecologism. Just because Green parties have views that cover the whole range of political and social life does not mean that they have Green views, in the sense of views that are strictly political-ecological. I suggest that Green parties typically draw their inspiration from the principles of political ecology rather than seeking fully to enunciate or enact them.

In this sense the word 'green' has been appropriated by many people who cannot be said to subscribe to a Green position at all. The title of John Elkington and Tom Burke's *The Green Capitalists* (1987), for example, has to be seen as a misnomer, if only because the book amounts to a hymn to material consumption that sits unhappily with the Green movement's prescriptions. Similarly, the idea that the major political parties have somehow turned green by peppering their manifestos with environmental promises is unsustainable – the Green movement's idea of the Good Life involves significantly more than fixing carbon dioxide scrubbers on industrial chimneys: 'we are . . . not in favour of a new industry to manufacture filters for the chimneys of power stations' writes Rudolf Bahro (1986, p. 18). It might be true to say that some of the movement's environmental initiatives have been adopted by the traditional parties, but this (as I have indicated above) makes very few inroads into the totality of Green ideology, properly understood. The Green agenda remains distinct.

Limits to growth

The need for the rethink of values advertised in this agenda is derived from the belief that there are natural limits to economic and population growth. It is important to stress the word 'natural' because Green ideologues argue that economic growth is prevented not for social reasons – such as restrictive relations of production – but because the Earth itself has a limited carrying capacity (for population), productive capacity (for resources of all types), and absorbent capacity (pollution). This ought to make it clear that from a Green perspective continuous growth cannot be achieved by overcoming what might appear to be temporary limits – such as those imposed by a lack of technological sophistication; continuous and unlimited growth is *prima facie* impossible. This theme will be pursued in Chapter 3.

At this point ecologism throws into relief a factor – the Earth itself – that has been present in all modern political ideologies but that has remained invisible, either because of its very ubiquity or because these ideologies' schema for description and prescription have kept it hidden. Ecologism makes the Earth as physical object the very foundation-stone of its intellectual edifice, arguing that its finitude is the basic reason why infinite population and economic growth are impossible and why, consequently, profound changes in our social and political behaviour need to take place. The enduring image of this finitude is a familiar picture taken by the cameras of Apollo 8 in 1968 showing a blue-white Earth suspended in space above the moon's horizon. Twenty years earlier the astronomer Fred Hoyle had written that, 'Once a photograph of the Earth, taken from the outside is available . . . a new idea as powerful as any other in history will be let loose' (in Myers, 1985, p. 21). He may have been right. The Green movement has adopted this

[15]

image and the sense of beauty and fragility that it represents to generate concern for the Earth, arguing that everyday life in industrial society has separated us from it: 'Those who live amid concrete, plastic, and computers can easily forget how fundamentally our well-being is linked to the land' (ibid., p. 22). We are urged to recognize what is and has always been the case: that all wealth (of all types) ultimately derives from the planet.

Sustainable societies

The centrality of the limits to growth thesis and the conclusions drawn from it lead political ecologists to suggest that radical changes in our social habits and practices are required. The kind of society that would incorporate these changes is often referred to by Greens as the 'sustainable society', and the fact that we are able to identify a Green society distinguishable from the preferred pictures of other ideologies is one of the reasons why ecologism can be seen as a political ideology in its own right.

I shall sketch what I understand the sustainable society to look like in Chapter 3, but one or two points about it should be borne in mind from the outset. Political ecologists will stress two points with regard to the sustainable society: one, that consumption of material goods by individuals in 'advanced industrial countries' should be reduced; and two (linked to the first), that human needs are not best satisfied by continual economic growth as we understand it today. Jonathon Porritt writes: 'If you want one simple contrast between green and conventional politics, it is our belief that quantitative demand must be *reduced*, not expanded' (1986, p. 136). It is obvious that if there are limits to growth then there are limits to consumption as well. The Green movement is therefore faced with the difficulty of simultaneously calling into question a major aspiration of most people – maximizing consumption of material objects – and making its position attractive.

There are two aspects to its strategy. On the one hand it argues that continued consumption at increasing levels is

[16]

impossible because of the finite productive limits imposed by the Earth. So it is argued that our aspiration to consume will be curtailed whether we like it or not: 'In common parlance that's known as having your cake and eating it, and it can't be done', announces Porritt (ibid., p. 118). It is very important to see that the Green movement argues that recycling or the use of renewable energy sources will not alone solve the problems posed by a finite Earth – we shall still not be able to produce or consume at an ever-increasing rate. Such techniques might be a part of the strategy for a sustainable society, but they do not materially affect the absolute limits to production and consumption in a finite system:

> The fiction of combining present levels of consumption with 'limitless recycling' is more characteristic of the technocratic vision than of an ecological one. Recycling itself uses resources, expands energy, creates thermal pollution; on the bottom line, it's just an industrial activity like all the others. Recycling is both useful and necessary – but it is an illusion to imagine that it provides any basic answers. (Porritt, 1986, p. 183)

This observation is the analogue of the distinction made earlier between environmentalism and ecologism. To paraphrase Porritt, the recycling of waste is an essential part of being Green but it is not the same thing as being Green. Being Green involves subscribing to different sets of values. As indicated by Porritt above, Greens are generally suspicious of purely technological solutions to environmental problems – the 'technological fix' – and the relatively cautious endorsement of recycling is just one instance of this. As long ago as the highly influential *The Limits to Growth* thesis it was suggested that 'We cannot expect technological solutions alone to get us out of this vicious circle' (Meadows *et al.*, 1974, p. 192) and this has since become a central dogma of Green politics.

The second strategy employed by Green ideologues to make palatable their recommendation for reduced consumption is to argue for the benefits of a less materialistic society. In the first place they make an (unoriginal) distinction between needs and wants, suggesting that many of the items we consume and that we consider to be needs are in fact wants that have been 'converted' into needs at the behest of powerful persuasive forces. In this sense they will suggest that little would be lost by possessing fewer objects. The distinction between needs and wants is highly controversial and will be considered in more detail in Chapter 3.

Secondly, the Green movement argues that the sustainable society that would replace the present consumer society would provide for wider and more profound forms of fulfilment than that provided by the consumption of material objects. This can profitably be seen as part of the Green contention that the sustainable society would be a spiritually fulfilling place in which to live. Indeed, the Green programme can hardly be understood without reference to the spiritual dimension on which (and in which) it likes to dwell. Greens invest the natural world with spiritual content and are ambivalent about what they see as mechanistic science's robbery of such content. They demand reverence for the Earth and a rediscovery of our links with it: 'It seems to me so obvious that without some huge groundswell of spiritual concern the transition to a more sustainable way of life remains utterly improbable' (Porritt, 1986, p. 210). In this way the advertisement for frugal living and the exhortation to connect with the Earth combine to produce the spiritual asceticism that is so much a part of political ecology.

A controversial theme in Green politics which is associated with the issue of reducing consumption is that of the need to bring down population levels. As Fritjof Capra explains: 'To slow down the rapid depletion of our natural resources, we need not only to abandon the idea of continuing economic growth, but to control the worldwide increase in population' (1985, p. 227). Despite heavy criticism, particularly from the left – Mike Simons has described Paul Ehrlich's proposals as 'an invitation to genocide' (*Green Line*, 64, July–August 1988, p. 13) – Greens have stuck to their belief that long-term global sustainability will involve reductions in population, principally on the grounds that fewer people will consume fewer objects: 'the only long-term way to reduce consumption is to stabilize and then reduce the number of consumers. The best resources policies are doomed to failure if not linked to population policy' (Irvine and Ponton, 1988, p. 29). Such a policy puts the Greens at odds with a number of European Economic Community member states that are concerned that the present tendency towards fewer births and smaller families poses the 'threat that there will be an excessive population of elderly persons' (*Guardian*, 11 January 1989, p. 8). Greens will argue that this is the necessary outcome of one of the steps required to provide us with a sustainable future.

Reasons for care for the environment

In an obvious way care for the environment is one of ecologism's informing (although not exhaustive) principles. Many different reasons can be given for why we should be more careful with the environment and I want to suggest that ecologism advances a specific mix of them. In this sense the nature of the arguments advanced for care for the environment by ecologism comes to be a part of its definition.

In our context such arguments can be summarized under two headings: those that suggest that human beings ought to care for the environment because it is in our interest to do so, and those that suggest that the environment has an intrinsic value that entitles it to existence regardless of the interest of human beings.

Most of the time we encounter arguments of the first sort; for example, that tropical rain forests should be preserved because they provide oxygen, or raw materials for medicines, or because they prevent landslides. These, though, are not fully Green reasons. The ecological perspective is neatly captured in *The Green Alternative* in response to the question, 'Isn't concern for nature and the environment actually concern for ourselves?':

[19]

Many people see themselves as enlightened when they argue that the nonhuman world ought to be preserved: (i) as a stockpile of genetic diversity for agricultural, medical and other purposes; (ii) as material for scientific study, for instance of our evolutionary origins; (iii) for recreation and (iv) for the opportunities it provides for aesthetic pleasure and spiritual inspiration. However, although enlightened, these reasons are all related to the instrumental value of the nonhuman world to humans. What is missing is any sense of a more impartial, biocentric – or biosphere-centred – view in which the nonhuman world is considered to be of intrinsic value. (Bunyard and Morgan-Grenville, 1987, p. 284)

Ecologism, then, appears to want to go beyond human-instrumental reasons for care for the natural world, arguing that the environment has an independent value that should guarantee its 'right to life'. Lurking behind this statement are complex issues, which will be discussed in detail in Chapter 2, but in this context of thinking about ecologism we need to make a distinction between the 'public' and the 'private' ecologist.

The private ecologist, in conversation with like-minded people, will most likely place the intrinsic value position ahead of the human-instrumental argument in terms of priority, suggesting that the latter is less worthy, less profoundly ecological, than the former. The public ecologist, however, keen to recruit, will almost certainly appeal first to the enlightened self-interest thesis and only move on to talk about intrinsic value once the first argument is firmly in place.

So the political ideology of ecologism clearly wants to subscribe to a particular set of reasons for care for the environment but is confronted by a culture that appears to engender a crisis of confidence, and that forces it to produce another set – which it would like to see as subordinate – in public. This, then, is another characteristic of ecologism: that its public face is in danger of hiding what it 'really' is, and yet what it 'really' is is its public face.

Something similar might be said of the spirituality that I have said often surfaces in the writings of ecologists. We have seen its advocates argue that Green politics is itself a spiritual experience in that it is founded on a recognition of the 'oneness' of creation and a subsequent 'reverence for one's own life, the life of others and the Earth itself' (Porritt, 1986, p. 111). Moreover, it is suggested that political change will involve such a recognition and that only Green politics has the possibility of re-creating the spiritual dimension of life that the grubby materialism of the industrial age has torn asunder. This kind of talk, though, is hardly a vote-winner and so although 'spirituality' might be conspicuous in the ecologist's private conversation it does not get the public airing that that would seem to warrant.

In this context another specific reason given for living 'in' the environment rather than against it deserves mention. It is suggested that the exploitation of the planet is linked to the exploitation of people, and that the ending of the former is a precondition for the ending of the latter. Lindy Williams, a former co-chair of the Green Party, writes that 'exploitation of the planet inevitably involves exploitation of people' (in Goldsmith and Hildyard, 1986, p. 360), and Norman Myers believes that 'we have the chance, quite simply, to be the first to live in final accord with our Spaceship Earth – and hence in final harmony with each other' (1985, p. 258).

These are strong claims to make. The only ground for making them would seem to be that exploitation is an attitude of mind, and that if we can persuade ourselves to abandon the most deep-rooted and unquestioned forms of exploitation – i.e. of the planet – then the liberation of people from exploitation will naturally follow. However, it is by no means obvious that the two forms of exploitation are linked. We can surely imagine a world in which populations live sustainably with respect to the environment, but exploitatively with respect to the social relations within those populations. Sustainable societies could take many forms and there seems no necessary reason why they should be any less exploitative of human beings than are present societies. The point here, though, is that political ecologists think that they will be, and for the specific reasons noted above.

[21]

Crisis and its political–strategic consequences

No presentation of Green ideology would be complete without the appropriate (usually heavy) dosage of warnings of doom and gloom. Political ecologists invariably claim that dire consequences will result if their warnings are not heeded and their prescriptions not followed. The *Limits to Growth* thesis provides a typical example:

> If the present growth trends in world population, industrialization, pollution, food production, and resource depletion continue unchanged, the limits to growth on this planet will be reached sometime within the next hundred years. The most probable result will be a rather sudden and uncontrollable decline in both population and industrial capacity. (Meadows *et al.*, 1974, p. 23)

The Green movement's consistent use of an apocalyptic tone is unique in the context of modern political ideologies, and it might be argued that the movement has relied too heavily on these sorts of projections as a means of galvanizing people to action. The consequences of this have been twofold. First, there is the unfounded accusation by the movement's critics that it is informed by an overwhelming sense of pessimism as to the prospects of the planet and the human race along with it. The accusation is unfounded because the movement's pessimism relates only to the likely life expectancy of current social and political practice. The Green movement is generally unerringly optimistic with respect to our chances of dealing with the crisis it believes it has uncovered – it merely argues that a major change of direction is required.

The second and perhaps more serious consequence of the movement's reliance on gloomy prognostications is that its ideologues appear to have felt themselves absolved from serious thinking about realizing the change they advertise. This, indeed, is another feature of the ideology that ought to be noted:

[22]

the tension between the radical nature of the social and political change that it seeks, and the reliance on traditional liberal–democratic means of bringing it about. It is as though the movement's advocates have felt that the message was so obvious that it only needed to be given for it to be acted upon. The obstacles to Green change have not been properly identified, and the result is an ideology that lacks an adequate programme for social and political transformation. Further comment on this will be made in Chapter 4.

Universality and social change

A related feature that ought to be mentioned, however, is the potentially universal appeal of the ideology. Up to now it has not been aimed at any particular section of society but is addressed to every single individual on the planet regardless of colour, gender, class, nationality, religious belief and so on. This is a function of the Green movement's argument that environmental degradation and the social dislocation that goes with it are everybody's problem and therefore ought to be everybody's concern: 'we are *all* harmed by the ecological crisis and therefore we *all* have a common interest in uniting together with people of *all* classes and *all* political allegiances to counter this mutually shared threat' (Tatchell in Dodds, 1988, p. 45; emphasis in the original). Ecologism thus has the potential to argue more easily than most modern political ideologies that it is, literally, in everyone's interest to follow its prescriptions.

This is not so obviously true of other modern political ideologies. None of them is able to argue that the penalty for not following its advice is the threat of major environmental and social dislocation for everyone. The potentially universal appeal generated by this observation has undoubtedly been seen by the Green movement as a positive characteristic, to be exploited for all it is worth. I shall examine this position in Chapter 4, and ask whether or not this belief is misplaced, and whether it has in fact rather been counterproductive in the sense of providing another reason for not attending sufficiently rigorously to the issue of social change.

Lessons from nature

The importance of nature to ecologism, already identified, is not exhausted by reasons why we should care for it. There is also a strong sense in which the natural world is taken as a model for the human world, and many of ecologism's prescriptions for political and social arrangements are derived from a particular view of how nature 'is'. This view – not surprisingly – is an ecological view. 'Professional ecologists', writes Jonathon Porritt, 'study plant and animal systems in relation to their environment, with particular emphasis on the inter-relations and interdependence between different life forms' (1986, p. 3). This characterization conveys the benign sense of nature that has been adopted by political ecologists. This is a natural world in which interdependence is given priority over competition and in which equality comes before hierarchy. Nature for ecologism is not 'red in tooth and claw' but pacific, tranquil, lush – and green.

The principal features of the natural world and the political and social conclusions or prescriptions that can be drawn from them are:

diversity	– toleration, stability and democracy
interdependence	– equality
longevity	– tradition
nature as 'female'	– a particular conception of feminism

These points will be discussed in greater detail in subsequent chapters, but some introductory remarks are in order here. First, it is an ecological axiom that stability in an ecosystem is a function of diversity in that ecosystem. Thus the more diverse the flora and fauna (within limits imposed by the ecosystem) the more stable the system will be. Further, stability is seen as

[24]

a positive feature of an ecosystem because it proves the system to be sustainable; an ecosystem that is subject to fluctuation has not reached the 'climax' stage and is therefore characterized as immature. Socially, this translates into the liberal aspiration of the toleration of peculiarity and generosity with respect to diverse opinions, and these are most certainly characteristics of liberalism that have been adopted by the Green movement. There is a strong sense in ecologism that the 'healthy society' (organic metaphor intended) is one in which a range of opinions is not only tolerated but celebrated, in that this provides for a repository of ideas and forms of behaviour from which to draw when confronted with political or social problems:

> Diversity must also be the codeword for the way we manage ourselves. Not only shall we need to draw from a wide range of cultural and minority options to improve the quality of our lives, but also to draw upon a broad, participatory power base in our political systems to oppose and reverse present trends towards homogeneity, over-centralization, the abuse of power, and an uncaring society. (Myers, 1985, p. 254)

It will be suggested later (in Chapter 3) that this aspiration stands in a tense relationship with the potential rigidity of norms and standards in a small-scale sustainable society. To this extent, ecologism encounters a similar problem to that found in the liberal tradition from which it draws: how to have a conception of the Good Society that requires people behaving in a certain way, and yet advertize for diverse forms of behaviour.

Nevertheless it is a Green maxim that dissenting voices be allowed to speak and in this sense ecologism subscribes to the democratic principle of government by consent. Nor is a vague sort of consent considered to be good enough: Greens argue for a radically participatory form of society in which discussion takes place and explicit consent is asked for and given across the widest possible range of political and social issues. All this implies the kind of decentralist politics associated with the

Green movement, which will be explored in greater detail in Chapter 3.

Some will no doubt object that this is too rosy a view of the Green movement's political prescriptions, and that its history is full of suggestions more accurately described as authoritarian than democratic. Anna Bramwell's history of ecology in the twentieth century (1989) certainly provokes such an impression, and it is true that even in the modern movement there was a time when avoiding environmental catastrophe was seen as the chief end, and the means used to achieve it were largely irrelevant:

> It [social design leading to a sustainable society] is a process that can be carried out within present authority structures whether they be democratic or dictatorial. It is not necessary, although it might be preferable, that authority relationships be changed. (Pirages, 1977b, p. 10)

This kind of agnosticism with respect to social organization was (and is) meat and drink to left critics of the Green movement who accused it of political irresponsibility and reaction. My belief now (confirmed by the content of this book), however, is that authoritarian solutions to the environmental crisis have been abandoned by the movement, and that it would therefore be quite wrong to see it in such a light.

This point is reinforced by ecologism's next political 'lesson from nature'. The view of the natural world as an interlocking system of interdependent objects (both sentient and non-sentient) generates a sense of equality, in that each item is held to be necessary for the viability of every other item. In this view no part of the natural world is independent and therefore no part can lay claim to 'superiority'. Without the humble bacteria that clean our gut wall, for example, human beings would be permanently ill. Likewise, those particular bacteria need our gut in which to live.

There is a sense, then, in which every relationship – from an ecological point of view – is a symbiotic relationship, and it is this that makes for a sense of equality. Moreover, this is a strong sense of equality in that it is held to be based on a directly observable principle of equality. There is no need to have recourse to abstractions (such as the 'thin' human being of liberalism) to generate it. From this point of view the boot is on the other foot as far as arguments about the possibility of equality are concerned. It has traditionally been a powerful anti-egalitarian position that, given the manifest inequality of human beings and species, the onus is on the egalitarians to show why they should be treated equally. Ecologists will argue that equality is at least as 'observable' as inequality and that therefore it is the inegalitarians who should shoulder the burden of persuasion. It might be objected, though, that interdependence need not necessarily imply equality – it is not hard to think of situations in which interdependence would probably be admitted but equality certainly would not: the relationship between a landlord and a villein for example, or between a working mother and her home help.

The fact of the longevity of the natural world is not, obviously, an observation specific to ecology, but nevertheless it has important ramifications for political ecologists. In a sense it is argued for the natural world that whatever is, is good, provided that it has not been meddled with by human beings with ideas above their station. Nature speaks with the wisdom born of long experience and attendance to 'her' lessons guarantees the best of all possible outcomes. The contrast between our puny modern knowledge and the tools it produces, and the rich vein of wisdom generated by forebears with an ear to the ground is clear: 'In modern farming the farm worker is increasingly isolated from the soil he is tilling; he sits encased in his tractor cab, either with ear muffs to shut out the noise or with radio blaring, and what goes on behind the tractor has more to do with the wonders of technology than with the wisdom of countless generations of his predecessors' (Bunyard and Morgan-Grenville, 1987, p. 71). As with farming, so with politics. Ecologists argue that we should live with, rather than

[27]

against, the natural world, and this has significant repercussions in the context of the kind of community in which they would have us live. At the same time, the natural world's longevity can help generate a sense of awe and humility and thus contribute to the move away from anthropocentrism that the Green movement considers necessary: 'The ecological approach . . . [introduces] an important note of humility and compassion into our understanding of our place on earth' (Eckersley, 1987, p. 10).

Not only, however, is nature held to be our best teacher, but 'she' is also female. This has important consequences for the feminism to which ecologism subscribes, because there is a tendency to map nature's beneficial characteristics on to the 'female personality'. Thus nature and women come to be tender, nurturing, caring, sensitive to place, and substantially defined by the (high) office of giving birth to life. To the extent that much feminist momentum has been geared towards ridding the woman of stereotypical behaviour and character patterns this ecological vision might seem retrograde. More pertinently, the features of this vision (if we assume women actually possess them to the general exclusion of other characteristics) are precisely those that have consigned women to an inferior status because they are held to be subordinate qualities. It will probably be of little comfort to some feminists that ecologism seeks to turn the tables in this context, arguing that the predominance of 'male' values is part of the reason for the crisis that they have identified, and that nature's 'female' lead is the one to follow. Brian Tokar puts it like this: 'The values of nurturance, cooperation and sharing which are traditionally identified more closely with women than with men need to become the deepest underlying principles of our society' (1987, p. 85). These are important matters both for ecologism and for feminism, both because ecologism claims feminism as a guiding star (not least in terms of how to 'do' politics), and because some feminists have balked at the kind of feminism shunted into ecological service. Much more will be made of this debate in Chapter 5.

Left and right; communism and capitalism

In standard political terms and in order to help distinguish ecologism from other political ideologies, it is useful to examine the widespread Green claim to 'go beyond' the left–right political spectrum: 'In calling for an ecological, nonviolent, nonexploitative society, the Greens (*die Grünen*) transcend the linear span of left-to-right' (Spretnak and Capra, 1985, p. 3). Jonathon Porritt translates this into a transcendence of capitalism and communism and remarks that 'the debate between the protagonists of capitalism and communism is about as uplifting as the dialogue between Tweedledum and Tweedledee' (Porritt, 1986, p. 44). The basis for this claim is that from a Green perspective the similarities between communism and capitalism are greater than their differences:

> Both are dedicated to industrial growth, to the expansion of the means of production, to a materialist ethic as the best means of meeting people's needs, and to unimpeded technological development. Both rely on increasing centralisation and large-scale bureaucratic control and co-ordination. From a viewpoint of narrow scientific rationalism, both insist that the planet is there to be conquered, that big is self-evidently beautiful, and that what cannot be measured is of no importance. (ibid., p. 44)

The name generally given to this way of life is 'industrialism', which Porritt goes so far as to call a 'super-ideology' within which communism and capitalism are inscribed, and which he describes elsewhere as 'adherence to the belief that human needs can only be met through the *permanent* expansion of the process of production and consumption' (in Goldsmith and Hildyard, 1986, pp. 343–4). This observation is central to Green ideology, pointing up both the focus of attack on contemporary politics and society – industrialism – and the claim that ecologism calls into question assumptions with which we have lived for at least two centuries. Ecologists argue that discussion about the

[29]

respective merits of communism and capitalism is rather like rearranging the deckchairs on the Titanic: they point out that industrialism suffers from the contradiction of undermining the very context in which it is possible, by unsustainably consuming a finite stock of resources in a world that does not have a limitless capacity to absorb the waste produced by the industrial process.

Although the Green movement appears to view 'left and right' and 'capitalism and communism' as synonymous pairs, I want to look at them separately, if only because the terms used to examine them will be different. It ought nevertheless to be said that the Green claim in both cases has come in for criticism, especially regarding the second pair, and especially from the left.

In some respects we can talk of the Green movement quite happily in terms of left and right because the terms we use to discuss the difference between the two can easily be applied to it. If, for example, we take equality and hierarchy as characteristics held to be praiseworthy within left-wing and right-wing thought respectively, then the Green movement is clearly left-wing, arguing as it does for forms of equality among human beings and between human beings and other species. However, to argue that ecologism is unequivocally left-wing is not so easy. For instance, Green politics is in principle averse to anything but the most timid engineering of the social and natural world by human beings. Since the French Revolution it has been a theme of left-wing thought that the existence of a concrete natural order of things with which human beings should conform and not tamper is a form of medieval mumbo-jumbo used by the right to secure and ossify privilege. The left has consistently argued that the world is there to be remade in the image of 'man' (usually) in accordance with plans drawn up by 'men' (usually), and in which the only reference to a natural order is to an abstract one outside of time and place.

The Green aspiration to insert the human being in its 'proper place' in the natural order and to generate a sense of humility in the face of it is clearly 'right-wing' in this context: 'The belief that we are "apart from" the rest of creation is an intrinsic feature of the dominant world-order, a man-centred or anthropocentric philosophy. Ecologists argue that this ultimately destructive belief must be rooted out and replaced with a life-centred or biocentric philosophy' (Porritt, 1984, p. 206). Ecologists can only perversely be accused of using this idea to preserve wealth and privilege, but the understanding of the place of the human being in a pre-ordained and immensely complex world with which we meddle at our peril is nevertheless a right-wing thought. Joe Weston, writing from a socialist perspective, puts it like this: 'Clearly the green analysis of environmental and social issues is within the broad framework of right-wing ideology and philosophy. The belief in "natural" limits to human achievement, the denial of class divisions and the Romantic view of "nature" all have their roots in the conservative and liberal political divisions' (1986, p. 24). Generally, the difficulty of describing ecologism as either obviously left- or right-wing is a legacy of its ambiguous relationship with the Enlightenment tradition referred to in the Introduction, and is consistent with its self-image of calling into question stock responses to that tradition.

Secondly, the Green claim to transcend capitalism and communism, in the sense that ecologism calls into question an overriding feature common to them both (industrialism), has drawn heavy criticism from the left. There are two reasons for this. In the first place it brings back grim memories of the 'end of ideology' thesis of the 1960s. This thesis has been interpreted by the left as itself ideological in the sense of observing a putative veneer of agreement about the basic goals of society, and so obscuring and illegitimatizing alternative strategies. The end of ideology position was buttressed by the convergence thesis, which argued that communist and capitalist nations were beginning to converge on a similar course of social and political action. The left pointed out that such analyses served to cement existing power relationships – particularly in the capitalist nations – and therefore performed a conservative social function.

So the left's belief that it is not possible to transcend capitalism while capitalism still exists makes it suspicious of claims to the contrary. David Pepper, for instance, has suggested that we should not see 'environmentalist concerns or arguments' as ' "above" or unrelated to traditional political concerns, but stemming from, and used very much as agents to advance, the interests of one traditional political side or the other' (1984, p. 187). The general conclusion that the left draws is that ecologism serves the interests of the status quo by diverting attention from the real battleground for social change: the relationship between capital and labour. We will be in a better position to assess the Green claim to transcend this battleground in Chapter 3 when ecologism's analysis and solutions to the crisis it identifies are set out, and I shall make more of ecologism's relationship with socialism in Chapter 5. The main point for now, though, is that it is undoubtedly a central feature of ecologism that it identifies the 'super-ideology' of industrialism as the thesis to be undermined, and it has been relatively easy for Green ideologues to point to high levels of environmental degradation in Eastern Europe to make their point that there is little to choose – from this perspective – between capitalism and communism. It makes no appreciable difference who owns the means of production if the production process itself is based on the assumption that its development need not be hindered by thoughts of limits to growth.

Historical specificity

Much of what has gone before leads me to the conclusion that we must understand Green, in a political sense, to be historically specific. This is to say that the historical situatedness of the Green movement becomes a part of the definition of its ideology. The point of this is, from one direction, to focus on the conditions necessary for bringing about the ideology I am describing; and from the other, to help demarcate its boundaries by excluding ideas and movements with which it has points of contact without being identical to them.

[32]

With respect to the first issue, there are obvious ways in which the fully developed ideology of the Green movement could not have existed up to now. It is clear, for instance, that the gloomy future predicted for us would have no persuasive purchase if damage to ecosystems had not reached levels that can sensibly be argued to be globally disruptive. Under its main front-page headline on 25 June 1988 the *Guardian* newspaper announced: 'As the United States buckles under the impact of the worst drought in 50 years, American scientists have confirmed that man-made pollutants are finally beginning to produce the long-predicted and potentially dangerous "green-house effect" on the world's climate.' Many will dispute this finding, but the important point is that it is not now an outrageous thing to say. If it were (and it would have been not so long ago), then ecologism would struggle to get off the ground.

Likewise the *Limits to Growth* report points out that, '*For the first time*, it has become vital to inquire into the cost of unrestricted material growth and to consider alternatives to its continuation' (Meadows *et al.*, 1974, p. 191; emphasis added). Similarly, the sense of survival urged upon us by the movement appears to assume greater relevance in the context of our very modern ability to destroy most of human life (at least) through nuclear war. In all of these cases certain preconditions for the emergence of ecologism have been provided by the present historical context, and in this sense the context becomes part of the ideology's definition.

It is evidently hard (and probably ill-advised) to try to be precise about dates in this respect: some will trace the beginning of the modern environmental movement back to the American conservationists of the nineteenth century, and some to the publication of Rachel Carson's *Silent Spring* in 1962, for instance. But it seems to me that the three ingredients necessary for the emergence of the ideology I am describing – namely a description of the limits to growth, the prescription of a fundamental change of political and social direction in response to this description, and the ready availability of the message to

[33]

a wide audience – first came together in 1972 with the publication of *The Limits to Growth* (although the studies that led to the book began in the summer of 1970). This is how the report expressed its principal conclusion: 'We are convinced that realization of the quantitative restraints of the world environment and of the tragic consequences of an overshoot is essential to the initiation of new forms of thinking that will lead to a fundamental revision of human behaviour and, by implication, of the entire fabric of present-day society' (ibid., p. 190). The sense of radical change advertised by the Green movement is captured in the final phrases of this quotation, and clearly goes beyond the managerial environmentalism that I am keen to separate from ecologism proper.

This, then, is the second way in which recognizing the historical situatedness of the ideology helps us to understand what it is. We are provided with a boundary beyond which (in the past) ecologism could not have existed, and therefore any movement or idea behind that boundary can bear only an informing relation to ecologism as I think we ought to understand it. Rachel Carson's book *Silent Spring*, then, can only inform ecologism rather than 'be' it because of the absence of an overriding political strategy for dealing with the problems it identifies. My suggestion is that, in 1962, ecologism (and therefore the possibility of being Green) did not exist, and that Rachel Carson's book and the period in which it was written are best viewed as part of the preconditions for ecologism. Looked at in this way we shall avoid the mistake made in many commentaries on and anthologies of socialism, say, which talk of the cleric John Ball (who spoke on behalf of the peasants during the rebellion of 1381) as if he were a socialist. The most that can be said of him, living as he did well before the French and Industrial revolutions that gave birth to socialism proper, was that his sentiments were socialistic. Similarly, the pre-1970 ideas and movements that have an affinity with ecologism are 'green' rather than Green.

The final important consequence of historicizing the ideology is that it enables us to emphasize the novelty of its analysis. It has been remarked that, despite its claims to the contrary, the Green movement's perspective is merely a reworking of old themes. Thus, for example, its warnings about population growth are substantially contained in the work of Thomas Malthus; its reluctance fully to embrace the mechanistic reason characteristic of the Enlightenment was a recurrent theme in the romantic movement of the nineteenth century; and even its apocalyptic tone has been prefigured on countless occasions in countless messianic movements. Such critics generally take these observations to indicate that, as has happened before, the subordinate themes associated with the Green movement will eventually be submerged by their dominant and opposed counterparts.

This interpretation fails to take full account of the historically specific nature of ecologism. For it is precisely the ideology's point that, while the terms of its analysis are not new in themselves, the fact of them being posited here and now gives those terms a novel resonance. So the critique of mechanical forms of reason, for instance, cannot be directly mapped back onto similar critiques made in the nineteenth century. The additional factor to be taken into account, argues the Green movement, is the potentially terminal state to which slavish usage of this reason has led us. In this way history defines the context within which ecologism operates (and therefore helps define ecologism itself), and provides the ground on which old themes acquire new resonances, coalescing to form a full-blown modern political ideology.

Conclusion

It needs to be stressed time and again that this is a book about ecologism and not about environmentalism. The reason that this needs to be stressed is that most people will understand environmentalism – a managerial approach to the environment within the context of present political and economic practices – to be what Green politics is about. I do not think it is.

Ecologists and environmentalists are both inspired to act by the environmental degradation they observe, but their strategies for remedying it differ wildly. Environmentalists do not necessarily subscribe to the limits to growth thesis, nor do they typically seek to dismantle 'industrialism'. They are unlikely to argue for the intrinsic value of the non-human environment and would balk at any suggestion that we (as a species) require 'metaphysical reconstruction' (Porritt, 1986, pp. 198–200). Environmentalists will typically believe that technology can solve the problems it creates, and will probably regard any suggestions that only 'frugal living' will provide for sustainability as wilful nonsense. In short, what passes for Green politics in the pages of today's newspapers is not the ideology of political ecology, properly understood. This is why the student of Green politics needs to scratch the surface of its public image in order to appreciate the full range of the debate that it has opened up.

CHAPTER 2

Philosophical foundations

We know that the white man does not understand our ways. He is a stranger who comes in the night, and takes from the land whatever he needs. The earth is not his friend, but his enemy, and when he's conquered it he moves on. He kidnaps the earth from his children. His appetite will devour the earth and leave behind a desert. If all the beasts were gone, we would die from a great loneliness of the spirit, for whatever happens to the beasts also happens to us. All things are connected. Whatever befalls the Earth, befalls the children of the Earth. (Chief Seattle, 1855; quoted in Bunyard and Morgan-Grenville, 1987, p. 3)

Central to the theoretical canon of Green politics is the belief that our social, political and economic problems are substantially caused by our intellectual relationship with the world and the practices that stem from it. The general targets of attack are those forms of thought that 'split things up' and study them in isolation, rather than those that 'leave them as they are' and study their interdependence. The best knowledge is held to be acquired not by the isolated examination of the parts of a system but by examining the way in which the parts interact. This act of synthesis, and the language of linkage and reciprocity in which it is expressed, is often handily collected in the term 'holism'. Thus holistic medicine is preferable to interventionist surgery, and ecology – which studies 'wholes' rather than 'parts' – is preferable to biology. Greater recognition of mutual dependence and influence, it is argued, will encourage a sensitivity in our dealings with the 'natural' world that discrete atomism has conspicuously failed to do.

[37]

Political ecologists often derive evidence for a holistic description of the universe from developments in physics during the twentieth century. It is no accident that one of the intellectual champions of the Green movement, Fritjof Capra (an Austrian now based in California), is a teacher and researcher of theoretical physics. His books, *The Tao of Physics* and *The Turning Point*, have had a tremendous impact within the movement and it is significant that Jonathon Porritt, the leading spokesperson for Green politics in Britain, should write of the latter: 'This is a brilliant book. Give yourself plenty of time for it . . . It was certainly a turning point for me' (1986, p. 242). It is the work of thinkers like Capra that gives the Green movement the confidence to claim that its world view is located at the sharp end of the latest thinking in science in general and physics in particular.

In this context, if twentieth-century physicists Niels Bohr and Werner Heisenberg are popular figures in the Green pantheon, then Francis Bacon, René Descartes and Isaac Newton are their complementary opposites. These three, according to the analysis of most Green theorists, produced a world view at variance in virtually all respects with that demanded by ecological survival in the twentieth century. Briefly, Bacon developed methods and goals for science that involved (and involve) the domination and control of nature; Descartes insisted that even the organic world (plants, animals etc.) was merely an extension of the general mechanical nature of the universe; and Newton held that the workings of this machine-universe could be understood by reducing it to a collection of 'solid, massy, hard, impenetrable, movable particles' (Newton, quoted in Capra, 1983, p. 52).

In contrast, twentieth-century physics' exploration of the subatomic world has led to a very different picture of the nature of the 'physical' universe. The Newtonian atomic description has given way to a universe in which (at the subatomic level at least) there are no solid objects, but rather fields of probability in which 'particles' have a tendency to exist. Nor are these 'particles' held to be definable in themselves: rather their nature is in their relationship with other parts of the system. As Niels Bohr commented: 'Isolated material particles are abstractions, their properties being definable and observable only through their interaction with other systems' (quoted in Capra, 1983, p. 69). Further, Werner Heisenberg's Uncertainty Principle (fundamental to the practice of quantum physics) shows that the observer – far from being independent of her or his experiment – is inextricably linked with it. Capra draws from this the requisite ecological–theoretical conclusion: 'We can never speak about nature without, at the same time, speaking about ourselves' (Capra, 1983, p. 77).

The differences between a seventeenth- and a twentieth-century description of the universe should be clear from this brief survey. The important similarity in our context, however, is that these descriptions have been used to generate, and then buttress, descriptions and prescriptions of how the *social* world is and ought to be. The 'bootstrap' interpretation of particle physics (that no one 'particle' is more or less 'fundamental' than any other) militates against hierarchy and works in favour of egalitarianism. Similarly, the fact that definitely bounded particles appear not to exist is held to count against atomistic pictures of society. As Capra and Charlene Spretnak have argued: 'Although Western culture has been dominated for several hundred years by a conceptualisation of our own bodies, the body politic, and the natural world as hierarchically arranged aggregates of discrete components, that world view is giving way to the systems view, which is supported by the most advanced discoveries of modern science and which is deeply ecological' (Spretnak and Capra, 1986, p. 29).

If twentieth-century physics provides ammunition against hierarchy and discreteness, then so does the science most obviously connected with the Green movement – ecology. At the same time, the science of ecology takes up the theme of egalitarianism implicit in the 'bootstrap theory' and adds a crucial ingredient: the apparently equal status of *species*. Any book on Green politics will tell you that the word 'ecology' was first used by the German biologist Ernest Haeckel in 1870, and that the science has to do, in Porritt's words, with 'the study

[of] animal and plant systems in relation to their environment' (1986, p. 3). The political implications of this study lie in the observation of the interrelationship and interdependence of these animal and plant systems, and, if one were to have to point to a basis for political ecology, then this would probably be it. It is from this notion of interdependence that the professed equality of value of species is generated.

Murray Bookchin presents the scientific picture of ecology in the following way:

> If we recognize that every ecosystem can also be viewed as a food web, we can think of it as a circular, interlacing nexus of plant–animal relationships (rather than as a stratified pyramid with man at the apex) that includes such widely varying creatures as microorganisms and large mammals. What ordinarily puzzles anyone who sees food-web diagrams for the first time is the impossibility of discerning a point of entry into the nexus. The web can be entered at any point and leads back to its point of departure without any apparent exit. Aside from the energy provided by sunlight (and dissipated by radiation), the system to all appearances is closed. Each species, be it a form of bacteria or deer, is knitted together in a network of interdependence, however indirect the links may be. A predator in the web is also prey, even if the 'lowliest' of the organisms merely makes it ill or helps to consume it after death. (Bookchin, 1982, p. 26)

Bookchin continues with a comment on the social implications of this: 'What renders social ecology so important is that it offers no case whatsoever for hierarchy in nature and society; it decisively challenges the very function of hierarchy as a stabilizing or ordering principle in *both* realms. The association of order as such with hierarchy is ruptured' (ibid., p. 36). In this way, the science of ecology works in favour of egalitarianism through its observations of the interdependence of species.

The kind of assertion made by Bookchin, however, is fraught with difficulties and I am saying nothing new – although the point bears repetition – if I suggest that extrapolations from 'nature' to 'society' are dangerous to make. It may be the case that the science of ecology has neutered hierarchy as an organizing principle in the 'natural' world (and this is, in any case, true with regard only to certain aspects of the natural world), but that is not to say that we can perform the same operation on it in the social world. The same point could be made with respect to egalitarianism, and the extrapolation becomes even less useful (for the Green movement) when we consider that equality in the 'natural' world itself is of a pretty poor quality. It is true that there is a measure of equality in that everything eats everything else, but some organisms get eaten more rapidly and more often than others. In other words, interdependence *can* be used to generate an egalitarian principle, but more work needs to be done on how such a principle works out in practice.

I shall return to this issue later in the chapter, but it ought to be pointed out now how the radical political ecologist would respond to this criticism. She or he would agree that the details of such a principle are hard to arrive at, but that the point of the principle is to encourage different ways of thinking about the 'natural' world. If we accept that a degree of inter-species equality of value is generated by the fact of our interdependence, then the onus will be upon those who want to destroy species to justify their case, rather than upon those who want to preserve them.

One further implication of the science of ecology, derived from its governing principle of interdependence, and which is central to the political ideology of ecologism, is its anti-anthropocentrism. If there is an identifiable equality of value of species then, as Bookchin suggests, the 'stratified pyramid with man at the apex' is not a presentable picture of the way things are. This, within the context of ecologism, is uncontroversial, and the issue of anthropocentrism itself will be dealt with later in the chapter. But I would like to take the opportunity presented by its mention to discuss a theory often referred to in ecological literature as a weapon in its intellectual armoury; namely, the Gaia hypothesis of James Lovelock. This theory is not as useful to the Green movement as it appears at first sight.

[41]

The Gaia hypothesis

In 1986, Lovelock described the thinking that had led him to advance his hypothesis fourteen years earlier:

> The Earth has remained a comfortable place for living organisms for the whole 3.5 billion years since life began, despite a 25% increase in the output of heat from the Sun. The atmosphere is an unstable mixture of reactive gases, yet its composition remains constant and breathable for long periods and for whoever happen to be the inhabitants. This, and other evidence that we live on 'the best of all possible worlds', was the basis of the Gaia hypothesis; living organisms have always, and actively, kept their planet fit for life. (Lovelock, 1986, p. 25)

The Gaia hypothesis (whose name was suggested by the Nobel prize-winning novelist, William Golding) has been the subject of considerable debate since Lovelock first presented it in 1972. Lovelock himself would be the first to admit that it has not gained total acceptance in the scientific community. Nevertheless, the reputability of the hypothesis can be judged by the fact that the debate surrounding it has taken place in some of the world's most prestigious scientific journals. Whether 'proved' or 'disproved', Lovelock's theory was soon seen by the Green movement to be potentially useful to its cause.

In the first place, its assertion that the planet is kept fit for life by the organisms that live on it bolsters the interdependence thesis, described above as central to both scientific and political ecology. This seems to me to be a legitimate conclusion, provided the theory is accepted in the first place. More specifically, and in terms of the debate over anthropocentrism, the hypothesis displaces human beings from the centre (or the apex, depending on the metaphor) of creation. It should be pointed out immediately, however, that Lovelock provides little encouragement for the egalitarians, because he suggests that some organisms are more important than others in keeping the planet fit for life: 'Gaia has vital organs at the core, as well as

[42]

expendable or redundant ones mainly on the periphery. What we do to our planet may depend greatly on where we do it' (Lovelock, 1979, p. 127). In fact he suggests that the continental shelves and the organisms living on them are most crucial to the planet's self-regulation as a supporter of life.

However, even if those who believe that all parts of the biosphere are of equal value get little joy from Lovelock, his hypothesis seems perfectly adequate for the general uses of the Green movement, and is often quoted in its popular literature: 'Lovelock's conception places humanity fair and square in its place among the rest of nature' (Bunyard and Morgan-Grenville, 1987, p. 279), and Porritt's 'Were such a hypothesis to be "proved", it would certainly put the kibosh on any lingering anthropocentric fantasies' (Porritt, 1986, p. 207). And quite apart from the damage that the Gaia hypothesis seems capable of doing to anthropocentrism, it is also able to underpin the kind of spiritual change that many ecologists feel to be necessary if we are to ensure our ecological survival. 'The spiritual implications of Gaia are profound' says one of Bunyard and Morgan-Grenville's contributors (1987, p. 280), and the implication is the sense of awe that Lovelock himself feels his hypothesis can produce – 'an alternative to that . . . depressing picture of our planet as a demented spaceship, forever travelling, driverless and purposeless, around an inner circle of the sun' (Lovelock, 1979, p. 12). The idea is that Gaia – the Earth – is a living being of immense complexity that ought to be the object of our wondrous contemplation, rather than the source of satisfaction for our rapacious material greed. The message is that Gaia deserves protection, and this is an anti-anthropocentric message in that it demands that we bury our projects if they prove harmful to the health of Gaia.

The problem with this is that the total health of Gaia – as Lovelock understands it – is not under threat. Lovelock argues that, 'On a planetary scale, life is near immortal' (Lovelock, 1986, p. 28), and suggests in his book that:

It is now generally accepted that man's industrial activities are fouling the nest and pose a threat to the total life of the planet which grows more ominous every year. Here, however, I part company with conventional thought. It may be that the white-hot rash of our technology will in the end prove destructive and painful for our own species, but the evidence for accepting that industrial activities either at their present level or in the immediate future may endanger the life of Gaia as a whole, is very weak indeed. (Lovelock, 1979, p. 107)

The question is: what does this mean for Porritt's 'kibosh on our anthropocentric fantasies'? It seems to me that if the Green movement insists on extracting the desired messages from the Gaia hypothesis (less growth, less pollution, less waste, etc.), then it can do so only by making either one or both of two moves. First, it can recast Lovelock's point and assert that it is *the present complexity* of Gaia (rather than Gaia as a total life-form) that deserves preservation; and/or, second, it can admit that the reason it asks us to abandon or modify our growth-oriented practices is not for Gaia's sake, but for our own.

The first option involves considerable embellishment of Lovelock's original thesis. His basic assertion (and the one that gives rise to awe and wonder), noted above, is that, 'The Earth has remained a comfortable place for living organisms for the whole 3.5 billion years since life began, despite a 25% increase in the output of heat from the sun'. He is not particularly concerned with the complexity of these organisms, or the relationships between them. The survival of Gaia does not depend on complexity, although it may be that the rapidity of its return to an equilibrium state is proportional to the degree of complexity of the life-forms that comprise it. Lovelock actually suggests that Gaia's health may depend on a reduction in complexity from time to time: 'any species that adversely affects the environment is doomed, but life goes on' (Lovelock, 1986, p. 28). In other words, Lovelock's hypothesis, as it stands, cannot be directly used to buttress Green (i.e. not human-providential) arguments against pollution, growth, and so on.

This leaves the alternative that we protect Gaia to protect ourselves – a very valid conclusion, but one that hardly 'puts the kibosh on our anthropocentric fantasies'. The warnings in Lovelock's hypothesis are far more serious for human beings than for Gaia. Lovelock suggests that we might be signing our own suicide note by continuing our industrial practices, in that the 'perturbations' that we, as a species, occasion in the atmosphere 'might trigger some compensatory change, perhaps in the climate, which would be good for the biosphere as a whole but bad for man as a species' (Lovelock, 1979, p. 9). So while the Gaia hypothesis might indeed lead us to contemplate our humble place in the grand scheme of things and thus to a 'decentring' of the human being, we quickly return to centre stage as humility turns into fear for survival.

This is because the uncomfortable corners of the Gaia hypothesis are uncomfortable for human beings, not for Gaia, and although Lovelock asserts that 'The philosophy of Gaia is not humanist' he immediately adds, 'but I cannot help being moved by thoughts about the future state of the Earth'. The reason he gives for this concern is the following: 'I have eight grandchildren and wish them to inherit a healthy planet' (Lovelock, 1986, p. 28). In this way, the inventor of the hypothesis extracts from it a human-providential reason for the care of Gaia, and this seems to me to be the only valid conclusion from the hypothesis as it stands. Consequently, the Green movement's adoption of the Gaia hypothesis betrays either woolly thinking or a latent anthropocentrism. I suspect that there are elements of both, but it is the latter that generates the most interesting discussion, as I hope to show nearer the end of the chapter.

Lastly, though, Lovelock's Gaia hypothesis might be read so as to provide no ammunition whatever for the Green movement – anthropocentrism notwithstanding. If Gaia is a self-regulating system, it might just be able to respond adequately to maintain the status quo (humans included) irrespective of what we throw at it. For example, it is now well known that the profligate burning of the Amazonian rainforest contributes

[45]

significantly to the build-up of carbon dioxide in the atmosphere both by releasing the gas during the burning process itself and by removing the principal absorbers of carbon dioxide – the trees themselves. Carbon dioxide is one of the so-called 'greenhouse gases', and it is feared that small percentage increases in its incidence might contribute to global warming, with all the disruption that that could cause.

Now, some sorts of cloud cover trap heat rising from the earth's surface, thus contributing further to the global warming phenomenon, but other sorts (particularly cirrus) reflect certain wavelengths of the sun's radiation before the rays ever reach the ground. Such clouds thus effectively 'cool' the earth. In this respect a Gaian regulatory response to our burning of the Amazon rainforest would be to increase cirrus cloud cover so as to restore average temperatures to the present equilibrium level. Experiments carried out to discover whether such increases have indeed taken place have proved inconclusive – not surprisingly, given the enormous complexity involved in modelling meteorological phenomena. Some evidence pointing towards increased cirrus has emerged however, and if this were to be confirmed and then shown to be a Gaian response, then Lovelock's Gaia hypothesis might just turn out to be a more potent weapon for the Green movement's opponents than for the movement itself. After all, if Gaia can absorb and regulate our environmental rapacity (without resorting to wiping us out) then it seems that our survival is not as obviously at stake as the Green movement would have us believe.

Whatever the implications of Gaia might be for the Green movement, the general thrust of the philosophy (or world view, to be less controversial) underpinning its politics is to dissolve the human in the 'natural' world – to, at the very least, *displace* the human being from its assumed position at the centre of creation. This enterprise has both its descriptive and its prescriptive aspects. The science of ecology, for example, suggests the actual existence of an inter-species dependence, and theoreticians in and around the Green movement argue that

[46]

this interdependence, and the responsibilities it carries with it, generate notions as to how human beings *ought* to behave. Consequently, human behaviour that belies this fact of interdependence will have a negative value, and it is to the ethical implications of this understanding of the relationship between human beings and the 'natural' world that I now turn.

Ethics: a code of conduct

A central concern of ecologism as a political ideology is the relationship between human beings and their environment. Consequently, almost all of what goes by the name of philosophy (or more often 'ecophilosophy') in the literature of ecologism has to do with describing that relationship and discussing its normative implications. More particularly, all forms of ecologism recommend restraint on the part of human beings with respect to their environment, and so ecophilosophy sees its task primarily in terms of the advancing of reasons for such restraint. It also seeks to judge between various reasons for restraint, and I shall suggest that not all reasons that can be given are radically ecological reasons, and that this leads to a distinction between what has come to be known as 'deep ecology', on the one hand, and the public face of ecologism as a political ideology, on the other.

The first influential use of the term 'deep ecology' is generally credited to the Norwegian, Arne Naess. In September 1972 Naess gave a lecture in Bucharest in which he drew a distinction between what he called the 'shallow' and the 'deep' ecology movements. The distinction had to do with the difference between a shallow concern at 'pollution and resource depletion', for the deleterious effects this might have on human life, and the deep concern – for its own sake – for ecological principles such as complexity, diversity and symbiosis (Naess, 1973, p. 95). I suggest that deep ecology informs Green politics in a way that will not be obvious to those who make Green

[47]

politics synonymous with environmentalism. Indeed, ecologism's being informed by deep ecology is precisely what (partly) helps distinguish it from environmentalism: environmentalists will be happy with shallow ecological reasons for care for the environment, while deep ecologists, although they will often make shallow ecological remarks, will probably feel uncomfortable as they do so. This is not to say that deep ecology is unproblematic from a political point of view, as I shall show.

Not surprisingly, the ethical content of ecophilosophy is overwhelming. Much ink has been spilt over issues such as the rights of animals, plants and wildernesses, and the duties that we as human beings might have towards them. In this context, the influence of the animal rights movement and its intellectual backers has been profound. It is largely true to say that the extension by the animal rights movement and its theorists of the ethical domain from humans to (some) animals has until recently been seen by ecophilosophers as the right course to pursue in their aim of producing an ethics for non-sentient nature.

The parentheses are necessary, however, because a number of ecophilosophers have dwelt on the difficulties of extending the work of animal rights theorists and sustaining a 'values-in-nature' (or 'intrinsic value') position (i.e. a position that would hold that all nature and not just some animals have intrinsic value), and have preferred to concentrate on the cultivation of a 'state of being' rather than a 'code of conduct' (Fox, 1986b, p. 4). This approach involves the belief that the development of an ecologically sound ethics is not possible within the current mode of ethical discourse (rights, duties, rational actors, the capacity for pain and suffering, and so on), and that such an ethics can only, and must, emerge from a new world view. Those who argue from this perspective point out that the current mode of discourse demands that ecologists present reasons why the natural world should *not* be interfered with. What is required, they suggest, is the cultivation of an alternative world view within which justifications would have to be produced as to why it *should* be interfered with (Fox, 1986a, p. 84).

[48]

Although Warwick Fox has hinted that the 'code of conduct' position is not as genuinely deep-ecological as the 'state of being' position (see the next section), there is no good reason why, for our purposes, we should divide them up in this way. The important point from the perspective of ecologism as a political ideology is that it seeks to persuade us that the 'natural' world has intrinsic value: that we should care for it not simply because this may be of benefit to us. Both the 'code of conduct' and the 'state of being' approaches want to arrive at that position, and to that extent their differences are tactical rather than strategic: they disagree as to how best to get there.

There is, then, a latent distinction in environmental ethics between, first, the attempt to develop an ethics from within the current mode of discourse, and second, the idea that such an ethics could only be produced from a more profound and general shift in ecological consciousness. Recently, this distinction has become explicit but, rather than begin with the current state of affairs, I propose to proceed historically. In dealing first with the attempt to develop an environmental ethic as an extension of the traditional debate, I hope to show some of the difficulties encountered, which the newer 'ecological consciousness' approach seeks to confront.

The first issue concerns just who or what this ethic ought to cover. Is it just sentient beings, as in Mary Midgley's desire in her book *Animals and Why They Matter* to treat 'all sentient beings as inside the moral community' (Midgley, 1983a, p. 89)? It is clear that this will not satisfy the Green movement because this is not an *environmental* ethic. But *The Green Alternative*'s first principle of deep ecology does not seem to go far enough either: 'All life has intrinsic value' (Bunyard and Morgan-Grenville, 1987, p. 281). What are we to understand by 'life'? Is not this too restrictive? What about rocks, deserts, and lakes?

Warwick Fox claims that the word is not too restrictive, but that our general understanding of it is. He chides Richard Sylvan for just such a misapprehension: 'It turns out that his definition of the term "biocentrism" restricts its application to biological life whereas deep ecologists have always used the term in a much broader sense to refer to an earth-centred (or "biospherical") perspective as opposed to a human-centred, sentience-centred or (biological) life-centred perspective' (Fox, 1986a, p. 7).

I do not think that deep ecology has been as free of discord on this topic as Fox implies, but that hardly matters here. The important point is that his version of 'biocentrism' takes us closer to that with which an environmental ethic would have to deal. Arne Naess also argues for an 'intuitive' notion of 'life' which can 'sometimes cover a stream, a landscape, a wilderness, a mountain, an arctic "waste" ' (Naess, 1984, pp. 202–3). But perhaps the classic statement of the reach of an environmental ethic has been provided by Aldo Leopold in his *A Sand County Almanac*:

> All ethics so far evolved rest upon a single premise: that the individual is a member of a community of interdependent parts. His instincts prompt him to compete for his place in that community, but his ethics prompt him also to co-operate (perhaps in order that there be a place to compete for).
>
> The land ethic simply enlarges the boundaries of the community to include soils, waters, plants, and animals, or collectively: the land. (Leopold, 1949, pp. 203–4)

This extension of the ethical community – the 'land ethic', as it has come to be known – has provided the starting point for environmental ethics ever since Leopold first formulated it.

One other important point that needs to be stressed again is that environmental ethicists who are true to the strictest interpretations of the world view of the Green movement have set themselves the goal of avoiding human-providential arguments for investing the environment with value. Thus, arguments that the non-human world should be preserved – because it is 'a stockpile of genetic diversity for agricultural, medical and other purposes'; 'for scientific study'; 'for recreation'; and 'for aesthetic pleasure/spiritual inspiration' (Fox, 1986b, p. 3) – are disqualified from environmental-ethical soundness by their anthropocentrism. It is this demand for a non-anthropocentric ethics that has caused so much difficulty, because it leads to confrontation with the issue of *intrinsic value*: 'We need an ethic that recognises the intrinsic value of all aspects of the nonhuman world' (Bunyard and Morgan-Grenville, 1987, p. 284). Thus, it is hoped, an ethical non-anthropocentrism will underpin responsible behaviour towards the non-human natural world.

What would intrinsic value look like? One way of looking at this would be to say that objects possessing such value 'would be held to have value independently of any awareness or appreciation of them or interest in them on the part of any conscious being' (Attfield, 1983, p. 146). This is a stiff condition and is immediately and obviously open to the subjectivists' objection that value is a quality invested in an object by human beings. In other words, objects are not the carriers of value; we are.

Several attempts have been made to counter this objection and to show that objects do carry value. Generally speaking, these attempts collapse into an appeal to our intuition – which of course by no means disqualifies them from consideration. Indeed, within the context of the Green movement itself, arguments from intuition carry at least as much weight as more traditional 'rational' approaches. For example, Holmes Rolston writes that, 'We can be thrilled by a hawk in a windswept sky, by the rings of Saturn, the falls of Yosemite'. He admits that 'All these experiences are mediated by our cultural education', but asserts that they 'have high elements of giveness, of finding something thrown at us, of successful observation' (Rolston, 1983, p. 144). Similarly, he says that, 'we have sometimes found values so intensely delivered that we have saved them wild, as in the Yellowstones, the Sierras and the Smokies' (ibid., p. 156). It is by no means the demand on our intuition that offends here, but that, while Rolston might persuade us to agree about the value of Nature's 'spectaculars', it might not stretch as far as other offerings such as the anopheles mosquito and the tsetse fly. Nevertheless, even if one can accept only that parts of the natural world have intrinsic value, some kind of a breach has been made in the subjectivists' argument.

Another favourite gambit of the intrinsic valuers is to ask us to conduct a thought experiment so as to test our susceptibility to their suggestions. The experiment can take many forms but the general idea is always the same. Consider, for example, Robin Attfield's version. Attfield asks us to think of the last surviving human being of a nuclear holocaust confronted by the last surviving elm tree. Attfield's question is: would this human being be doing anything wrong in cutting down the elm tree, knowing that she or he would die before the tree? He reports that 'most people who consider this question conclude that his [sic] act would be wrong' (Attfield, 1983, p. 155), and that this is evidence of a visceral feeling for intrinsic value. His rationalization of this effect is that trees have a 'good of their own' and 'are thus at least serious candidates for moral standing' (ibid., p. 145).

The rationalization works less well than the appeal to emotion and intuition, and this is not surprising. As Mary Midgley has pointed out, the intellectual principles of traditional morality isolate 'the duties which people owe each other *merely as thinkers* from those deeper and more general ones which they owe each other as beings who feel' (Midgley, 1983b, p. 170). This applies equally well to the relationship between human beings and the 'natural' world and, to this extent, environmental ethics has to satisfy the emotions as well as the intellect. In this context, Attfield's and Rolston's appeal to intuition is perfectly justifiable; Rolston is well aware, in any case, that 'Resolute subjectivists cannot . . . be defeated by argument' (Rolston, 1983, p. 157).

However, the appeal to intuition (for those who are not satisfied by it) is not the only avenue open to value-objectivists. A very interesting alternative has been put forward by Stephen Clark in his article 'Gaia and the forms of life'. He begins with a general move against value-subjectivists by arguing, uncontroversially and not originally, that their position only gets off the ground if they agree on 'something, if it is only the life of reason, as objectively valuable' (Clark, 1983, p. 191). The idea is that value-subjectivists have to see value in reason, for it is reason upon which their value-subjective argument is based. But how is this going to help those arguing for intrinsic value in the 'natural' world? As Clark says: 'It is at this point that rationalists of all persuasions have halted: very well, it is a necessary postulate of human reason that reason be respected, but we do not similarly need to postulate that the world, the nonhuman, the nonrational, be respected' (ibid.).

The next step, though, is the crucial one, as Clark suggests that 'If we really set ourselves to disown and devalue the sentiments and structure of our mere animal humanity we shall find ourselves adrift' (ibid.). To continue the metaphor, Clark is arguing that our intellect, our rationality, floats on a sea of 'animal humanity', living in the sensuous world. To respect reason is to respect that which sustains it – the world in which we live. Clark concludes: 'we can only take ourselves seriously by taking the web, the system, the whole of which we are a part, with similar seriousness. To despise, to reconstruct, to poison, that whole is to destroy ourselves, not only for the strictly practical reasons that I have already sketched [i.e. damage to the environment is damage to ourselves] but also because it is a self-contradiction' (ibid., p. 192).

The rationalist kind of strategy employed by Clark to counter the value-subjectivists is not well represented in the literature concerning intrinsic value. The appeal to intuition is much more common. Clark's approach, however, has two major advantages. First, it operates from within the accepted philosophical discourse in that his anti-value-subjectivist argument is a variant on the standard critique of truth-relativism: if truth is relative then there is no point in the truth-relativist ever arguing for the truth of his or her position. The advantage of working with accepted currency is tactical: a more sympathetic hearing is likely to be given to the case for intrinsic value if no great demands are made on the listener's accustomed form of debate. Clark's second advantage is that his perspective ascribes

[53]

intrinsic value right across the non-human world, with none of the problems of anopheles mosquitoes and tsetse flies associated with Rolston's intuitive approach, described above.

The problem with Clark's approach, however, from a deep ecological point of view, is its apparent anthropocentrism. Reason, as we generally understand it, is a peculiarly human faculty, so to ascribe intrinsic value to the non-human world via the avoidance of rational self-contradiction might seem overly human-centred. It should be pointed out, however, that this is a different kind of anthropocentrism from the human-instrumental variety – Clark is not ascribing value to the non-human world on the basis of the benefits that might accrue to us by so doing, but simply in terms of what it is to be a human being. This observation, and particularly the distinction between two types of anthropocentrism that it involves (i.e. human-centred and human-instrumental), will be taken up later in the chapter.

The problems of environmental ethics are, however, by no means confined to the problem of intrinsic value itself. Having argued a case for intrinsic value in the non-human world, one is then committed to describing to whom or what it is to be attached: individuals in the biotic community? groups of such individuals (e.g. species)? ecological concepts, such as diversity and symbiosis? Nor is this question merely scholastic – on its answer turns the resolution of conflicts that may arise between these different 'ecological subjects'.

Various approaches have been made on the issue of the 'ecological subject', although it is not always clear that their champions are aware of the consequences of plumping for one or the other, or of the possible contradictions between them. Warwick Fox, for example, has talked of the intrinsic value of 'the nonhuman members of the biotic community' (Fox, 1984, p. 194), while Arne Naess refers us to 'principles of diversity and symbiosis' (Naess, 1973, p. 96). *The Green Alternative* states that, 'Symbiosis with diversity together form the complexity of nature – a vast world of relationships, connections and possibilities. There is intrinsic value in this crystal web of complexity' (Bunyard and Morgan-Grenville, 1987, p. 281); while the Routleys argue for intrinsic value in 'Diversity of systems and creatures, naturalness, integrity of systems, harmony of systems' (in Thompson, 1983, p. 90), and Devall and Sessions refer to 'richness and diversity of life forms' as being 'values in themselves' (in Spretnak and Capra, 1985, p. 233).

There is clearly the possibility that these principles will come into conflict. For example, a wolf pack (group) will operate more effectively without an injured member (individual), and Attfield has pointed out, while considering the 'Gaian' argument that the biosphere as a whole has moral standing, that 'there can be a conflict between maximising its excellences and maximising the intrinsic value of its components' (Attfield, 1983, p. 159). As an extreme example (for us), we might remember Lovelock's warning that Gaia would probably be better off without the human race. As far as conflicts concerning principles such as diversity and complexity are concerned, it might be argued that the disappearance of the human race would contribute to the *diversity* of the biosphere because of the reprieve of the species that would have been destroyed had we stayed around. However, our demise would also involve a reduction in *complexity* since it would mean the disappearance of what is possibly the most complex discrete organism in the biosphere.

In short, the problems of resolving conflicts between the claims of different 'ecological subjects' have proved very awkward. Even if we restrict ourselves to trying to find solutions to conflicts between species (i.e. *within* a given 'ecological subject'), the complications are formidable. This is one problem within environmental ethics that has received great attention, and it surfaced very early on, as a result of Naess's 'Principle Two' of deep ecology, described in his seminal 1973 paper. The idea is: 'Biospherical egalitarianism – in principle' (1973, p. 95). The difficulty with this becomes clear if one focuses on the small-print clause 'in principle', and Naess's own comment upon it: 'The "in principle" clause is inserted because any realistic praxis necessitates some killing, exploitation and suppression' (ibid.). This has become a famous phrase in environmental-ethical literature – how much killing? and who or what is to be exploited and suppressed?

The notion of biospherical egalitarianism is evidently problematic. Mary Midgley caustically rejects the principle of an 'equal right to live and blossom' when she says that biospherical egalitarians

> have . . . made things extremely hard for themselves lately by talking in a very wholesale, *a priori*, French-revolutionary sort of way about all animals being equal, and denouncing 'species-ism' as being an irrational form of discrimination, comparable to racism. This way of thinking is hard to apply convincingly to locusts, hookworms and spirochaetes, and was invented without much attention to them. (Midgley, 1983a, p. 26)

So how are problems of conflict to be resolved? How is the 'in principle' clause to be filled out? Various attempts at a resolution have been made, all necessarily revolving around the construction of a hierarchy of organisms. In this context, complexity is a favourite datum. For instance, in 1984, in a formulation that I suspect he would now renounce, Warwick Fox explicitly related value to complexity in the following way:

> To the extent that value inheres in complexity of relations, and to the extent that complexity of relations is evidenced in the degree of an organism's central organisation (and therefore for capacity of richness of experience), then organisms are entitled to moral consideration commensurate with their degree of central organisation (or capacity for richness of experience) for the duration of their existence. (Fox, 1984, p. 199)

He goes on: 'Recognising this, we should be clear that the central intuition of deep ecology does not entail the view that intrinsic value is spread evenly across the membership of the biotic community' (ibid.). Now this evidently makes rather a mess of the principle of biospherical egalitarianism: it is in fact a principle of biospherical inegalitarianism.

In this way, attempts to solve the difficulties with Naess's principle have ended by undermining the principle itself. This is clear evidence of the intractability of the problem – and it is an absolutely practical problem for the politics of the Green movement. Anyone who has drowned slugs in a cup of beer to stop them eating the lettuces may be congratulated on a certain ecological sensibility, but was the action environmentally ethical? As Richard Sylvan has commented: 'The guidelines as regards day-to-day living and action for a follower of deep ecology remain unduly and unfortunately obscure' (Sylvan, 1984b, p. 13).

It is these difficulties and obscurities that have led some practitioners of environmental ethics effectively to abandon attempts to develop one within the current mode of discourse. By 1986, for example, Warwick Fox is asserting that biospherical egalitarianism 'operates at a lower level of definiteness than a value theory, i.e. it refers to the general attitude *underlying* what we recognise as specific ethical decisions and practices' (Fox, 1986, p. 40). This is the issue to which I referred earlier as the shift from the developing of a 'code of conduct' to that of a 'state of being'. It is to this that I now turn.

Ethics: a state of being

There was a time, then, when deep ecology was associated primarily with the belief that the non-human world could have (and did have) intrinsic value. This appeared to be a radical move within traditional ethical discourse, with far-reaching practical implications for the relationship between human beings and their environment. In ethical terms it was (and is) an attempt to move beyond human-prudential arguments for concern for the biosphere.

But, as I have indicated, a number of deep ecology theorists began to balk at the difficulties associated with developing a cast-iron intrinsic value theory. This has led them to propose the necessity for an ethics proceeding from a changed state of

[57]

consciousness, rather than hoping that it might be developed from within the present dominant one. Some of these latter theorists have argued that deep ecology has always been a 'consciousness first, ethics later' enterprise. I believe this to be wrong, although that hardly matters here. What there has always been is a mixture of the two, but it is only relatively recently that the problems encountered with 'values-in-nature' have led to the explicit separation of a 'state of being' and a 'code of conduct'.

Warwick Fox, for example, insists that the attempt to develop intrinsic value from Naess's principle of biospherical egalitarianism involves a 'misinterpretation' of the principle, and admits that he was a 'party to it' (1986a, p. 37). But can so many people have been so wrong? I think, rather, that it was a fair interpretation of the principle, but one that has been found wanting. As a result of the difficulties with intrinsic value, some theorists have chosen to place it on the back burner while emphasizing the metaphysics of deep ecology. I must stress again that the metaphysics has not suddenly been invented to cope with the intrinsic value obstacle, as some participants seem to suggest (e.g. Richard Sylvan in his two *Radical Philosophy* articles and 1984a, p. 2, in particular), but nor has it always performed the same foundational function that it now does for some deep ecologists.

This distinction between a 'state of being' and a 'code of conduct' has led, in some quarters, to the disqualification of intrinsic valuers from the deep ecology camp. This is the move made by Warwick Fox in his talk given to the Fourth National Environmental Education Conference in Australia in September 1986. Basing himself on work by John Rodman, Fox distinguished between 'four general kinds of environ-mentalist approaches', the last two of which he described as 'intrinsic value theory' and 'deep ecology' (Fox, 1986b, p. 2). This distinction has the effect of disengaging deep ecology from a 'values-in-nature' position whereas, certainly in Naess's original 1973 article at least, the ethics and the metaphysics are presented together with no clear foundational distinction.

The 'state of being' position begins from the following sort of premise: that an 'ecological consciousness connects the individual to the larger world' (Bunyard and Morgan-Grenville, 1987, p. 282). This 'ecological consciousness' serves as a new foundation on which a different (ecological) ethics and new (ecological) forms of behaviour would be built. The idea involves the cultivation of a sense of self that extends beyond the individual understood in terms of its isolated corporal identity. To this is added the notion that the enrichment of self depends upon the widest possible identification with the non-human world. Naess puts this in the following way:

> Self-realisation cannot develop far without sharing joys and sorrows with others, or more fundamentally, without the development of the narrow ego of the small child into the comprehensive structure of a Self that comprises all human beings. The ecological movement – as many earlier philo-sophical movements – takes a step further and asks for a development such that there is a deep identification of all individuals with life. (In Fox, 1986a, p. 55)

Ecological consciousness, then, has to do with our identification with the non-human world, and the understanding that our self-realization is presaged upon such identification, and the behaviour that would logically result. It is not hard to see how an environmentally sound ethic emerges from this. Fox writes, 'For example, when asked why he does not plough the ground, the Nez Perce American Indian Smohalla does not reply with a closely reasoned explanation as to why the ground has intrinsic value but rather with a rhetorical question expressive of a deep identification with the earth: "Shall I take a knife and tear my mother's breast?" ' (Fox, 1986a, p. 76). In other words, the ethics issues 'naturally' from an alternative vision of reality, and this is the reason for the rejection of the primacy of ethics: 'I'm not much interested in ethics and morals,' writes Naess, 'I'm interested in how we experience the world . . . If deep ecology is deep it must relate to our fundamental beliefs, not just to

[59]

ethics. Ethics follows from how we experience the world. If you experience the world so and so then you don't kill' (in Fox, 1986a, p. 46).

Now there are at least three points to be made about this notion of ecological consciousness and its implications. In the first place: how far does it involve a reversion to the original sin of anthropocentrism? It seems clear that the principle of self-realization described above, although it generates concern for the non-human world, generates it for human-providential reasons. To this extent, the development of an ecological consciousness as foundational to an environmental ethics may avoid the problems associated with producing the latter from conventional discourse, but at the cost of diluting the non-anthropocentrism that is held to be central to an ecological perspective.

The second point revolves around the problem of potential conflicts between human interests and the interests of the environment, discussed in another context above. One can imagine an immensely wide identification of my 'self' with the non-human world, but still see the survival of my own self as dependent upon a certain amount of 'killing, exploitation and suppression' of that non-human world. Where does that leave the practical implementation of the new ethics that might arise from an 'ecological consciousness'? It certainly seems that Richard Sylvan's demand for 'guidelines as regards day-to-day living' is not satisfied by anything in the ecological consciousness approach. Nor is this a problem confined to some putative 'pre-ecological consciousness era'. There is no suggestion made by this set of deep ecologists that, once a general ecological consciousness has been attained, problems of environmental conflict will 'wither away'. Indeed, Warwick Fox recognizes that conflict between human beings and the non-human world is inevitable: 'my "small" self must meet certain vital needs even at the expense of the vital needs of other (relatively autonomous) entities' (Fox, 1986a, p. 58). No guidelines are produced, however, for deciding between various sets of 'vital needs', or for deciding what they might be.

[60]

The deep ecologists' answer to this objection is that they are in the business not of providing a rule-book, but of advancing a consciousness of identification with the non-human world that would markedly alter the conditions within which any rule-book would be written. Fox makes the point cogently:

> in terms of preserving the nonhuman world, the wider identification approach is more advantageous than the environmental axiological approach in a political or strategic sense because it shifts the onus for justification of one's actions from the person who wants to preserve the nonhuman world to the person who wants to disrupt or interfere with it. (Fox, 1986a, p. 84)

I think that this is a genuinely significant point to make, and it would certainly have an effect on the environmental ethic that might emerge. Problems of conflict would, of course, remain, but the degree of conflict would be considerably reduced. There is no question but that the non-human world would benefit from a general instilling of an 'environmental consciousness', such as Fox and others have described it. Shifting the onus of justification in this way does not absolve us, of course, from drawing lines of legitimate environmental intervention, but it does mean that the lines will be drawn in very different territory from that which emerges if the onus of justification is not shifted. Put differently, if it is preservation of the non-human world that has to be justified then more environmental intervention is likely to be countenanced than if it is intervention that has to be justified.

However, the next problem – and this is the third point – concerns the generation of this 'wider identification' in people. How are they to be convinced of it? If Robert Aitken is correct when he says that 'Deep ecology . . . requires openness to the black bear, becoming truly intimate with the black bear, so that honey dribbles down your fur coat as you catch the bus to work' (in Fox, 1986a, p. 59), then deep ecology would seem to be in deep trouble. The guffaws that generally greet statements such

[61]

as Aitken's reveal deep ecology's profound problem of persuasion.

To explain: those who now choose to advance the claims of a 'state of being' over a new 'code of conduct' were forced into this position by what they saw as a sense of realism – it was understood that traditional ethical concepts could not do the environmental work required of them. Put another way, they asked: where does an ethics come from? and came up with the answer: from a given understanding of the way the world is; a metaphysics. The conclusion was to argue for a change in metaphysical perspective towards that described in the first part of this chapter, on the understanding that the desired environmental ethic would be more likely to flourish in this new climate.

However, the metaphysics advanced by deep ecology is (to say the least) taking its time getting a grip, and the self-identification with the non-human world demanded by it is restricted – in 'advanced industrial countries' at least – to isolated pockets of well-meaning radicals. Deep ecology has asked: where does the ethics come from? and has answered: from a metaphysics. But its long-term problem may lie in finding an answer to the question: where does the metaphysics come from? because here lies the clue to why the advocacy of a change of consciousness, on its own, is not sufficient. Consciousness is not an independent datum, isolated from the social conditions that nurture it.

Janna Thompson gets closest to the remark that needs to be made: 'Ethical resolution . . . presupposes social critique: an attempt to show that present social relations and the goals and desires that spring from them, are unsatisfactory, and that new conceptions of self-fulfillment and happiness are desirable' (Thompson, 1983, p. 98). This social critique ought to be part and parcel of the deep ecological enterprise, but the eco-philosophers write as though the resolution of philosophical problems were enough to bring about the resolution of practical problems, such as pollution, deforestation and acid rain. Normally, indeed, the social and political context receives no attention at all. Warwick Fox writes: 'This attempt to shift the *primary* focus of environmental philosophical concern from ethics to ontology clearly constitutes a fundamental or revolutionary challenge to normal environmental philosophy. It is (and should be) deep ecology's guiding star' (Fox, 1984, p. 204). If deep ecology is content to remain in the territory of theory, then Fox may be right in his identification of its 'guiding star'. But if it is concerned to turn the theory into practice, it will have to present a programme for social change. This it has so far failed to do.

Anthropocentrism

If there is one word that underpins the whole range of Green objections to current forms of human behaviour in the world, it is probably 'anthropocentrism'. Concern for ourselves at the expense of concern for the non-human world is held to be a basic cause of environmental degradation and potential disaster. On the one hand, however, the very centrality of this word to the Green cause has led to a muddying of its meaning; while on the other, the practical issue of getting the Green ideology across has led to contradictory messages from its theorists about anthropocentrism.

As regards the first point, I want to suggest that there is a strong and a weak meaning for the word – meanings that emerge from a reading of the ecophilosophical literature, but that are rarely formally distinguished. My understanding of the weak meaning is referred to by Warwick Fox as having to do with being 'human-centred' (Fox, 1986b, p. 1). What I call the strong meaning also comes from Fox, and involves seeing 'the nonhuman world purely as a means to human ends' (Fox, 1984, p. 198). We might refer to these positions as 'human-centred' and 'human-instrumental', respectively. Both of these descriptions were used by Fox with explicit reference to anthropocentrism, but they clearly have different implications. The first, or weak, sense is more obviously 'neutral' than the second, or strong, sense. The strong sense carries a notion of the injustice and unfairness involved in the instrumental use of the non-human world. I want to suggest that anthropocentrism in the weak sense is an unavoidable feature of the human condition. This will not do damage to the ecologists' case; in fact it enables them unashamedly to put the human onto the ecological agenda – an agenda from which, for reasons associated with its aims, the centrality of the human being has all but been erased.

The dangers of such erasure have become clear in the theoretical stances and political activities of the North American group Earth First!, a group that has been referred to as 'deep ecology's political action wing' (Reed, 1988, p. 21), and 'the cutting edge of environmentalism' in the American west (Tokar, 1988, p. 134). One article in an Earth First! journal (engagingly signed Miss Ann Thropy) stated that, 'If radical environmentalists were to invent a disease to bring human population back to sanity, it would probably be something like Aids . . . the possible benefits of this to the environment are staggering . . . just as the Plague contributed to the demise of feudalism, Aids has the potential to end industrialism' (quoted in Reed, 1988, p. 21). Neither is the group all words and no action. Some time ago Earth First! took to driving nails into the trunks of Californian redwood trees to deter loggers from cutting them down, and at least one lumberjack has been badly injured by his chainsaw kicking out of the trunk and into his neck.

It would be a mistake to think that deep ecology necessarily leads to Earth First!-type activities and so to reject it on that basis. Chris Reed's assertion (in the article referred to above) that 'Descent into irrationality has badly damaged American feminism', and that 'The present uproar among environmentalists seems only too likely to repeat the feminists' mistake' (ibid.) not only is misguidedly offensive to radical feminism but is also a one-sided reading of the implications of deep ecology. For example, shifting the onus of justification from those who would preserve the non-human world to those who would intervene in it (presented above as implied by deep ecology) hardly justifies the kind of disciplinary violence practised by some members of Earth First!

Be that as it may, the reintroduction of the human onto the Green political agenda in a non-anthropocentric way is essential, and so the accusation of anthropocentrism in the strong sense identified above does damage to an ecologist's case, if we accept the ground rule that the reasons given for care for the non-human world are as important as the care itself. What the self-respecting ecologist has to avoid is a human-instrumental reason. As we shall see shortly, however, this is precisely the sort of reason for changes in behaviour often advanced by the ideologues of ecologism.

In the literature, one finds the weak and strong meanings of anthropocentrism mixed together – sometimes in the same sentence. Richard Sylvan, for example, defines as anthropocentrism any attitude that 'does not move outside a human-centred framework, which construes nature and the environment instrumentally, that is, simply as a means to human ends and values' (Sylvan, 1984a, p. 5). To my mind, and contrary to Sylvan's implication, a 'human-centred framework' does not necessarily mean that it is human-'instrumental'. Consider, for example, the following statement from Jonathon Porritt: 'For us, it is not enough to protect animals for practical, self-interested reasons alone; there is also a profoundly moral concern, rooted in our philosophy of respect for all that dwells on the planet' (Porritt, 1986, p. 184). The first half of the sentence represents a rejection of human-instrumentalism, while the second half involves human-centredness ('our philosophy of respect'). There is no contradiction in this, but it does show that there is room for a (weak) form of anthropocentrism in respectable ecological statements.

The reason for this is that weak anthropocentrism is a necessary feature of the human condition. As Tim O'Riordan has pointed out, 'Man's conscious actions are anthropocentric by definition. Whether he seeks to establish a system of biotic rights or to transform a forest into a residential suburb, the act is conceived by man in the context of his social and political culture' (1981, p. 11). It is this factor that links even the search for intrinsic value with anthropocentrism. The search is a *human* search, and although it may be successful in displacing the human being from centre-stage in terms of value, one will always find a human being at the centre of the enterprise, asking the questions. If there were no human beings there would be no such conceptualized thing as intrinsic value, and it is an open question whether there would be any such thing as intrinsic value at all. In this sense, any human undertaking will be (weakly) anthropocentric, including the Green movement itself.

The reason for dwelling on this is that the Green movement may be doing itself a disservice by what has been seen as its insistent distancing from the human. In the first place it is self-contradictory. Charlene Spretnak, for example, writes that, 'Green politics rejects the anthropocentric orientation of humanism, a philosophy which posits that humans have the ability to confront and solve the many problems we face by applying human reason and by rearranging the natural world and the interactions of men and women so that human life will prosper' (Spretnak and Capra, 1985, p. 234). There is evidently a quite correct rejection of human–instrumentalism here, but also a disturbing hint that human beings should abandon their pretensions to solving the problems they have brought upon themselves. This suspicion is reinforced by comments of the following kind: 'In the long run, Nature is in control' (ibid.). If Spretnak really believes this, one wonders why she bothers to write books persuading us of the merits of Green politics. The fact of her involvement implies a belief that she has some control, however minimal, over the destiny of the planet.

Overall, of course, it is the generalized belief in the possibility of change that makes the Green movement a properly political movement. Without such a belief, the movement's reason for being would be undermined. From this perspective, the recognition that weak anthropocentrism is unavoidable may act as a useful political corrective to the idea that 'Nature is in control': at least it reintroduces the human onto the agenda – a necessary condition for there to be such a thing as politics.

Indeed, when it comes to the politics of the Green movement, as opposed to its philosophy, there is generally little reluctance to indulge in anthropocentrism – even of the strong variety. In *Green Politics*, for example, Capra and Spretnak talk of 'an understanding that we are part of nature, not above it, and that all our massive structures of commerce – and life itself – ultimately depend on wise, respectful interaction with our biosphere'. And if that is not a clear enough expression of a human-prudential argument, the authors add: 'Any government or economic system that ignores that principle is ultimately leading humankind into suicide' (1985, p. 28).

Again, Jonathon Porritt writes that the 'ecological imperative . . . reminds us that the protection of the Earth's natural systems is something we all depend on', and that 'The fact that thousands of species will disappear by the turn of the century is not just an academic irritation: our own survival depends on our understanding of the intricate webs of life in which we're involved' (1986, pp. 98–9). In fact, Porritt goes as far as to make human-instrumentalism the lever for engineering the changes that ecologism recommends: 'A re-interpretation of enlightened self-interest is . . . the key to any radical transformation' (ibid., p. 117).

The same strong anthropocentric message comes through loud and clear in Green Party manifestos. In the section entitled 'Environment and Nature', the German Greens' manifesto states that: 'Encroachment on natural habitats and the extermination of animal and plant species is destroying the balance of nature *and along with it the basis of our own life*. It is necessary to maintain or restore a biologically intact environment, *in order to ensure the humane survival of future generations* (*German Green Party Manifesto*, 1983, p. 29; emphasis added). And on the next page we find a perfect expression of the strong anthropocentric principle: 'We must stop the violation of nature in order to survive in it' (ibid., p. 30).

[67]

The British Green Party's manifesto is less explicit but equally clear: 'The relentless pursuit of economic growth has brought *humankind* to the brink of a disaster which is unprecedented in history' (1987, PB [Philosophical Basis] 101; emphasis added), and: 'The overriding, unifying principle is that all *human* activities must be indefinitely sustainable' (PB 303), with the answer to the question: sustainable for whom? supplied by the italicized words.

The list of examples is endless, and they all demonstrate the same point: that the politics of ecology does not follow the same ground rules as its philosophy. I suggested earlier in the chapter that, for ecophilosophers, the reasons for the care of the non-human world are at least as important as the care itself. For ecophilosophers, care should be disinterested. This principle appears to have been abandoned (or at least suspended) by the majority of the Green movement's political ideologues.

Several reasons for this might be advanced, among which is the reason of convenience – i.e. that for the purposes of communicating the basic idea of care for the 'natural' world, short-cuts may have to be taken. This is the approach outlined by Warwick Fox in the following lengthy but worthwhile quote:

> Consider the following. If you ask me to try to tell the 'average person' in one sentence why I think we ought to care about some nonhuman 'being' (whether alive or not), then the simplest thing for me to say, given our present cultural context, is along the lines: 'Because it has all these uses for us'. However, if I wish to get a little closer to what I really want to say, but at the same time take care to speak in terms that others will immediately understand rather than in terms that might sound alien to them (and, hence, alienate them), then I will probably say something along the lines: 'Because it has value in itself'. Unless we have a lot more time to talk, the last thing I am going to say *given the present cultural context* is the first thing I want to say: 'Because it is part of my/our wider Self; its diminishment is My/Our diminishment'. In other words, given the constraints of culture, desire to persuade, and limited time

in which to try to communicate something clearly, my *popular* statement of 'basic principles' will, while reflecting my deepest views, nevertheless be an unreliable or superficial guide to the way in which I would elaborate these views in formal, philosophical terms. (Fox, 1986a, pp. 71–2)

On this reading, the purveyors of human-providential reasons for the care of 'nature' can always say that they do so only for tactical reasons – that the end of persuasion is more important than the means of achieving it. At one level this collapses into an issue of the intellectual consistency of individuals, but at another, a profoundly important political question is raised: will human-providential reasons do the job for the environment that is required of them? Put another way: does the use of human-providential reasons (as means) endanger the desired end of a 'hands-off' approach to the environment?

Presumably the answer of 'ecological consciousness' supporters to these questions would be, respectively: no and yes. The whole point of developing a perspective which goes beyond (what I have defined as) a strong anthropocentric principle is that such a principle only serves to reinforce the attitude which the Green movement is concerned to invalidate – that which has the universe revolving around the human being. Warwick Fox's persuasive argument is that only the development of an ecological consciousness will turn the tables in favour of the environment, such that the onus of persuasion is on those who want to destroy, rather than on those who want to preserve. Now, if this is the end towards which the Green movement is aiming, it is hard to see the merits of an approach which undermines it. The best that can be said of human-providentialists, from the point of view of the deep ecologists, is that they will get some of the job done, albeit at the cost of ditching the totality of the enterprise.

I think it would be wrong to jump to the conclusion, however, that this disagreement counts towards a disqualification of ecologism's political ideologues from the ecological camp. My strong sense, in any case, is that, although political ecologists might publicly give human-instrumental reasons for care for the environment, they are likely to have been motivated to do so by considerations of the intrinsic value variety. There is little point in trying to draw up a definitive list of requirements for deep ecological membership. Much more interestingly, the differences between the philosophy of deep ecology and its political manifestation are symptomatic of a failure of the philosophy to make itself practical.

I should mention in passing that this failure has accounted for some famous political casualties – none more so than Rudolf Bahro, who left the German Green Party in June 1985 over the issue of animal experimentation. Bahro's position was one of uncompromising opposition to animal experimentation, for recognizably deep ecological reasons. He complained that the German Green Party

> has no basic ecological position; it is not a party for the protection of life and I know now that it never will be, for it is rapidly distancing itself from that position. Yesterday, on the question of animal experiments, it clearly came down in favour of the position taken by the speaker who said, more or less: 'If even one human life can be saved, the torture of animals is permissible'. This sentence expresses the basic principle by which human beings are exterminating plants, animals and finally themselves. (Bahro, 1986, p. 210)

The sentence Bahro quotes also expresses a form of strong anthropocentrism that would be rejected by deep ecologists. The German Green Party's acceptance of the principle of animal experiments, and Bahro's consequent departure from the Party, are a concrete expression of ecophilosophy's failure to make itself practical.

Nor do I mean by this simply that the recommendations of ecophilosophy are impractical or Utopian. I want to make the more far-reaching point that ecophilosophy has not paid enough attention to the practical relations among people, and

between people and their environment, that make its recommendations impractical. Perhaps I can make this clearer by
referring to Karl Marx's Eighth Thesis on Feuerbach, which
runs as follows: 'Social life is essentially *practical*. All mysteries
which mislead theory to mysticism find their rational solution
in human practice and in the comprehension of this practice' (in
Feuer, 1976, p. 285).

While not wanting to endorse everything Marx has to say, I
think Marx's thought here points us in the right direction. The
idea is that there are things about the world that are hard to
understand ('mysteries'), and that their resolution can take on
an inadequate theoretical form ('mysticism'). In our present
context, I would argue that the environmental crisis is the
'mystery' and that ecophilosophy – in all its various forms – is
the 'mysticism'. Marx's thesis goes on to point out that
adequate understanding lies in the comprehension of the social
life and its practices that give rise to the problem, or 'mystery'.
Further, that the tendency towards 'mystical' solutions is a
function of those very forms of social life (i.e. the present ones),
and thus that both the avoidance of 'mysticism' and the final
resolution of the 'mystery' will depend upon changes in social
practice. If this is correct, and if I am justified in interpreting
ecophilosophy in this light, then ecophilosophy's failure to
address the issue of social practice will disqualify it from ever
formulating a satisfactory solution to the problems that have
given rise to it.

This is what I meant when I said above that 'the differences
between the philosophy of deep ecology and its political
manifestation are symptomatic of a failure of the philosophy to
make itself practical'. This is not to say that ecophilosophy's
embracing of the practical would immediately resolve all
conflicts of theory or practice, but it would make radical
disagreements of the type that forced Bahro to leave the German
Green Party unlikely. The reason is that a practical philosophy
would have a strategy for social change built into it, a programme around which activists could work and within which
disagreements would be over tactics and not over strategy.

[71]

The 'changes in social practice' to which I have just referred are very much conceived within the ecology movement to be the concern of its political, rather than its philosophical 'wing'. It is this tendency towards the separation of the theoretical from the practical – or, better, the refusal explicitly to link them – that I would criticize in ecophilosophy. However, if it is also true to say that successful practical resolutions are associated with successful theoretical resolutions, then the lacunae in ecophilosophy will have profound practical (political) ramifications. Discussion of this point will take us both further into this book (see Chapter 4), and towards the heart of ecologism as a political ideology.

CHAPTER 3

The sustainable society

Greens have sought to separate surface symptoms from the root causes of our growing problems. They have spotlighted the direction society must take if it wants a sustainable and satisfying future: partnership with the rest of nature, 'soft technology, "steady state" economics, human-scale institutions and a population size within the environment's long-term carrying capacity' (Irvine and Ponton, 1988, p. 3)

Limits to growth

Amid the welter of enthusiasm for lead-free petrol and green consumerism it is often forgotten that the foundation-stone of Green politics is the belief that our finite Earth places limits on industrial growth. This finitude, and the scarcity it implies, is an article of faith for Green ideologues, and it provides the fundamental framework within which any putative picture of a Green society must be drawn. The guiding principle of such a society is that of 'sustainability', and the stress on finitude and the careful negotiation of Utopia that it seems to demand, forces political ecologists to call into question green consumerist-type strategies for environmental responsibility. In this respect it is principally the limits to growth thesis, and the conclusions drawn from it, that divides light-green from dark-Green politics.

An enormous quantity of material has already been produced that reflects on the limits to growth issue, and I do not see it as my task here to rehearse the arguments to which the notion has given rise. I do think it important, though, to stress its centrality to the Green position, and to take this opportunity to point out the features of the limits to growth thesis that are most often referred to in Green discussions. Greens have all along been confronted with rebuffs to their belief in limits to growth, and as their responses to these criticisms have developed it has become easier to identify what they are prepared to jettison in the thesis and what they feel the need to defend.

It turns out that there are three principal thoughts related to the limits to growth thesis that have come to be of prime importance to the Green position. They are, first: that technological solutions (broadly understood; i.e. solutions formulated substantially within the bounds of present economic, social and political practices) will not bring about a sustainable society; second: that the rapid rates of growth aimed for (and often achieved) by industrialized and industrializing societies have an exponential character, which means that dangers stored up over a relatively long period of time can very suddenly have a catastrophic effect; and third: the issues associated with the interaction of problems caused by growth – i.e. that solving one problem does not solve the rest, and may even exacerbate them. These three notions will be discussed in more detail very shortly, but first (principally for the uninitiated) the strategy and conclusions of the original *Limits to Growth* report ought briefly to be noted.

The researchers pointed to what they described as '5 trends of global concern': 'accelerating industrialisation, rapid population growth, widespread malnutrition, depletion of nonrenewable resources, and a deteriorating environment' (Meadows *et al.*, 1983, p. 21). They then created a computerized world model of the variables associated with these areas of concern, i.e. industrial output per capita, population, food per capita, resources and pollution, and programmed the computer to produce pictures of various future states of affairs given changes in these variables. From the very beginning it was understood that such modelling would be rough and ready, and the Club of

Rome (the name given to the informal association of scientists, researchers, industrialists etc. that carried out the research) anticipated later criticisms of inaccuracy and incompleteness by admitting that the model was 'imperfect, oversimplified and unfinished' (ibid., p. 21). From our perspective, the important point to make is that the Green movement has been generally unperturbed by criticisms of the detail of the various limits to growth reports, and has rather built itself upon the general principles and conclusions of these reports.

The first computer run, then, assumed 'no major change in the physical, economic, or social relationships that have historically governed the development of the world system' (ibid., p. 124). This, in other words, was a run in which business carried on as usual. In this case the limits to growth were reached 'because of nonrenewable resource depletion' (ibid., p. 125). Next, the group programmed a run in which the resource depletion problem was 'solved' by assuming a doubling in the amount of resources economically available. In this case collapse occurred again, but this time because of the pollution brought about by the spurt in industrialization caused by the availability of new resources. The group concluded that, 'Apparently the economic impetus such resource availability provides must be accompanied by curbs on pollution if a collapse of the world system is to be avoided' (ibid., p. 133). Consequently, the next computer run involved not only a doubling of resources but also a series of technological strategies to reduce the level of pollution to one-quarter of its pre-1970 level (ibid., p. 136). This time the limits to growth are reached because of a food shortage produced by pressure on arable land owing to its being taken for 'urban–industrial use' (ibid., p. 137).

And so the experiment progressed, with the world model programmed each time to deal with the immediate cause of the previous collapse. Eventually all sectors have technological responses filled in:

The model system is producing nuclear power, recycling resources, and mining the most remote reserves; witholding as

[75]

many pollutants as possible; pushing yields from the land to undreamed-of heights; and producing only children who are actively wanted by their parents. (ibid., p. 141)

Even this does not solve the problem of overshoot and collapse:

> The result is still an end to growth before the year 2100. In this case growth is stopped by three simultaneous crises. Overuse of land leads to erosion, and food production drops. Resources are severely depleted by a prosperous world population (but not as prosperous as the present [1970] US population). Pollution rises, drops then rises again dramatically, causing a further decrease in food production and a sudden rise in the death rate . . .

and the next sentence of the group's conclusion on the computer's final run helps distance environmentalism from ecologism and provides the intellectual springboard for Green political strategy: 'The application of technological solutions alone has prolonged the period of population and industrial growth, but it has not removed the ultimate limits to that growth' (ibid., p. 141).

This, then, brings us to the first of the three notions associated with the limits to growth thesis that I suggested above are essential to the theory and practice of political ecology: that technological solutions cannot provide a way out of the impasse of the impossibility of aspiring to infinite growth in a finite system. Irvine and Ponton point out that 'technological gadgets merely shift the problem around, often at the expense of more energy and material inputs and therefore more pollution. Favourite devices such as refuse incineration, sulphur extractors in power stations and catalytic convertors in cars cost money and energy while at the same time generating new pollutants' (1988, p. 36). This will most likely appear heretical to those familiar with light-green, environmental politics, which bases itself precisely upon this sort of strategy, but it is at just these points that ecologism distinguishes itself most clearly from environmentalism.

[76]

So if the sustainable society is not, on the face of it, going to be full of environment-friendly technological wizardry, then how does it begin to distinguish itself from present practices? Part of the answer is provided by Garrett Hardin's definition of a 'technological solution': 'one that requires only a change in the techniques of the natural sciences, demanding little or nothing in the way of change in human values or ideas of morality' (quoted in Meadows *et al.*, 1983, p. 150). It follows that if the Green movement believes technological solutions to the limits to growth problem to be impossible, then it will have to argue for more profound changes in social thought and practice – changes in human values and ideas of morality. These changes will involve accommodating social practices to the limits that surround them, and abandoning the Promethean (in this context, technological) attempt to overcome them. It is in this kind of respect, once again, that the Green sustainable society is different from the green environmentalist one, and why the latter can sit only uncomfortably with the former. All of this is a result of the idea that technological solutions can have 'no impact on the *essential* problem, which is exponential growth in a finite and complex system' (ibid., p. 45).

And this is the second notion that political ecologists have rescued from the debate over limits to growth, making it central to their argument as to why present industrial practices are unsustainable: the notion of exponential growth. Meadows *et al.* claim that all of the five elements in the Club of Rome's world model experience exponential growth, and explain that 'A quantity exhibits *exponential* growth when it increases by a constant percentage of the whole in a constant time period' (ibid., p. 25). In quantitative terms this is easily demonstrated by placing rice grains on the squares of a chess board, with one on the first square, two on the second, four on the third, sixteen on the fourth, and so on. The numbers build up very fast and while the twenty-first square will be covered with over 100,000 grains of rice, the fortieth will require about 1 million million (ibid., p. 29).

The central point is that such growth is deceptive in that it produces large numbers very quickly. Translated to the arena of industrial production, resource depletion and pollution, what seems an innocuous rate of use and waste disposal can quickly produce dangerously low quantities of available resources and dangerously high levels of pollution. Greens often point to the staggeringly rapid growth in industrial production this century and ask the (increasingly less rhetorical) question: can this be sustained? Thus Irvine and Ponton note that, 'In a mere blink on the timescale of human evolution, industrial society has been depleting and impairing Earth's "supply system" at a phenomenal rate', and that, 'Americans, for example, have used more minerals and fossil fuels during the past half-century than all the other peoples of the world throughout human history' (1988, pp. 24–5).

Greens believe, simply, that present rates of resource extraction and use – a '3% growth rate implies doubling the rate of production and consumption every twenty-five years' (Ekins, 1986, p. 9) – and the production of waste and pollution necessarily associated with it, are unsustainable. They further believe that the nature of the rate of growth produces a false sense of complacency: what appears to be a safe situation now can very quickly turn into an unsafe one. A relevant French riddle for schoolchildren goes like this:

> Suppose you own a pond on which a water lily is growing. The lily plant doubles in size each day. If the lily were allowed to grow unchecked, it would completely cover the pond in 30 days, choking off the other forms of life in the water. For a long time the lily plant seems small, and so you decide not to worry about cutting it back until it covers half the pond. On what day will that be? On the twenty-ninth day, of course. You have one day to save your pond. (Meadows *et al.*, 1983, p. 29)

The third and final aspect of the limits to growth thesis that has become central to the Green position is that of the interrelationship of the problems with which we are confronted. It should already have become clear from the description of the Club of Rome's computer runs above that solving one problem apparently does not necessarily mean

[78]

solving the rest, and our refusal to confront the complexity of the global system and to draw the right conclusions for action (or inaction) from it is why most Greens believe our attempts to deal with environmental degradation, in particular, to be insensitively inadequate. 'What matters', write Irvine and Ponton, 'is not any particular limit, which might be overcome, but the total interaction of constraints, and costs' (1988, p. 13). Change in one element means change in the others: nuclear power might contribute to solving problems of acid rain but it still contributes to global warming, and chemical fertilizers help us grow more food but simultaneously poison the water courses.

Fundamentally this is a problem of knowledge, in the context of which Green ideologues adopt a predominantly conservative stance: 'One of the worst changes that industrialism has made to pollution is not the addition of individual new pollutants, but their combined effects . . . Some half a million chemicals are in common use; about another thousand are added each year. Yet we know next to nothing about their interaction and combined effects, and the scale of the problem suggests that we never will' (Irvine and Ponton, 1988, p. 34). The implied impossibility of knowing enough is crucial to the Green suggestion that we adopt a hands-off approach to the environment. If we cannot know the outcome of an intervention in the environment but suspect that it might be dangerous, then we are best advised, from a Green point of view, not to intervene at all. In this respect Green politics places itself firmly against drawing-board design and thus in the realm of what is generally considered to be conservative politics – siding with Edmund Burke against Tom Paine, so to speak.

So Greens read off three principal features of the limits to growth message, and subscribe to them and their implications wholeheartedly: technological solutions cannot help realize the impossible dream of infinite growth in a finite system; the exponential nature of that growth both founds its unsustainability and suggests that the limits to growth may become visible rather quicker than we might think; and the immense complexity of the global system leads Greens to suggest that our present attempts to deal with environmental problems are both clumsy and superficial.

Underpinning all this, of course, is the most profound belief of all: that there *are* limits to growth. The most common criticism of the *Limits to Growth* report is that its predictions as to the likely exhaustion of raw materials (for example) have been proved wildly wrong. Greens have learned to accept the detail of these criticisms while continuing to subscribe to the general principle of the limits to growth thesis. Thus a contributor to Bunyard and Morgan-Grenville's compilation recognizes that the original report underestimated both the amount of resource reserves to be discovered and the ability of the system to cope in terms of the production of synthetic substitutes, etc., but continues: 'The simple fact is that if we go on using up the earth's nonrenewable resources (its oil, coal, minerals) at the rate we are now, and misusing the earth's renewable resources (its fertile soil, clear water, forests) at the rate we do now, then at some stage in the future the whole system is going to fall apart' (1987, p. 327).

This is the starting-point for thoughts about the sustainable society: that aspirations of ever-increasing growth and consumption cannot be fulfilled because, 'To spread such [American] consumption levels to the rest of the world's expanding numbers would require over 130 times the world output of 1979' (Irvine and Ponton, 1988, p. 25). Thus, 'The concept of scarcity is fundamental . . . It is rooted in the biophysical realities of a finite planet, ruled and limited by entropy and ecology' (ibid., p. 26). Green politics is founded upon a fundamental commitment to the principle of scarcity as an insurmountable fact of life and the consequent limits to growth imposed by a finite system. In this respect, to hint that Green political thought is damaged by hitching itself to the *Limits to Growth* report – because of its self-fulfilling prophecy of doom, programmed to collapse by dint of Malthusian reasoning – is rather to miss the point. Green thinkers just do believe that present industrial practices are programmed to collapse by virtue of their internal logic, and in this respect they are persuaded by the fundamental message of the limits to growth thesis.

It is worth stressing here a point made in the Introduction: that this 'scientific' element in the Green position pushes it well beyond a merely romantic response to the trials and tribulations of industrial society. Greens advertise for a sustainable society not merely because they think, in terms of some bucolic fantasy, that it would be more pleasant to live in. They believe that science is on their side. The first Law of Thermodynamics states that 'we do not produce or consume anything, we merely rearrange it' – so we cannot produce resources, we can only use them, and they will eventually run out. The second Law – that of entropy – has it that 'our rearrangement implies a continual reduction in potential for further use within the system as a whole' (Daly, 1977b, p. 109). This also implies that there is a limit to the use we can make of scarce resources, as well as pointing out that waste (high entropy) is a necessary product of the extraction and use of resources (low entropy). The limits to growth notion is thus the practical reason, as it were, why Greens argue for the necessity of a sustainable society. They also present 'social' and 'ethical' reasons (Daly in Ekins, 1986, p. 13), which will be pursued as the chapter progresses. Now, though, we are in a position to sketch the parameters within which Greens believe any picture of the sustainable society would have to be drawn.

Possible positions

Various responses to the problem of sustainability are available, both in political–institutional terms and also in terms of the social and ethical practices that a sustainable society would need to follow. By no means all of the 'solutions' that have been presented over the years are Green in the sense in which I think we ought to understand the word – i.e. in the sense in which ecologism has become a political ideology in its own right. In drawing the boundaries for ecologism, we find ourselves excluding from its meaning a number of political postures that have been wrongly associated with it. This has the effect, of course, of narrowing down the range of thoughts and practices that we can link with Green politics, and thus makes clearer the territory within which it most properly moves.

To my mind no one in this context has been able to (or has had to) improve upon the typology provided by Tim O'Riordan in his book *Environmentalism* (1981, pp. 303–7). O'Riordan suggests that in political–institutional terms there are four principal postures available. First, there is the possibility of a 'new global order', arranged so as to deal with the problems of global coordination presented by the international nature of the environmental crisis. Supporters of this position typically claim that the nation-state is both too big and too small to deal effectively with global problems and bemoan the lack of efficacy of the United Nations, which, nevertheless, seems to be the kind of organization on which they would base their new global order. O'Riordan refers to people like Barbara Ward and René Dubos (*Only One Earth*) as supporters of this view, to whom we might now add Gro Harlem Brundtland, ex-Prime Minister of Norway, after her *Brundtland Report* of 1987.

The second position is described as 'centralized authoritarianism'. This position also takes seriously the existence of an environmental crisis, and its supporters believe that, because no one is likely to succumb voluntarily to the measures needed to deal with it, they will have to be made to do so. The locus of authority is generally seen as the governments of nation-states, and in this respect no major political–institutional changes are held to be necessary. Governments would merely decide upon a course of action leading to sustainability (perhaps protectionism, rationing, population control and restriction on immigration) and would put it into effect regardless of opposition. O'Riordan refers to William Ophuls ('whatever its specific form, the politics of the sustainable society seem likely to move us along the spectrum from libertarianism toward authoritarianism' – 1977, p. 161) and Garrett Hardin as exemplars of this position.

The third posture described by O'Riordan is that of the 'authoritarian commune', which is principally differentiated from the previous position by the scale on which the sustainable society would operate. Institutional structures would be broken down, the locus of decision-making would (in principle) be devolved, but social structures would, of necessity, remain hierarchical. The model, says O'Riordan, is that of the Chinese commune, and he also refers to Heilbroner's *An Enquiry into the Human Prospect* as a prototype for this kind of thinking. Some might put Edward Goldsmith, co-author of *A Blueprint for Survival* (1972) and editor of the *Ecologist*, in this bracket, but although he appears traditionally hierarchical in some respects – particularly in the context of relations within the family – his support (for example) for forms of participatory democracy disqualifies him from full membership of the authoritarian commune canon.

The final possibility referred to by O'Riordan in his typology is the 'anarchist solution'. He makes his meaning clearer by writing that, 'The classic ecocentric proposal is the self-reliant community modelled on anarchist lines' (1981, p. 307). This shares the commune perspective with the previous position and thus envisages a major shift in the focus of authority and decision-making, but differs from it in adopting a left-liberal stance on relations within the community. In political terms at least (and often in material terms as well), O'Riordan's 'anarchist solution' is fundamentally egalitarian and participatory.

Now, not all of these presentations can accurately be described as corresponding to the political ideology of ecologism. They are all, of course, responses to a perceived environmental crisis, and to this extent they all have something to do with the notion of a sustainable society, but they do not by any means all paint pictures of what we ought to understand by a *Green* sustainable society. Briefly, the closest approximation of the four positions described above to the centre of gravity of a Green sustainable society is the last one: the so-called 'anarchist solution'. It should be stressed that in adopting O'Riordan's typology I do not want to suggest that the Green solution is itself an anarchist solution. We can say only that the

[83]

sustainable society has certain characteristics that enable us to describe it as 'anarchistic'.

The importance of all this is that apologists for the Green society will gain their inspiration from the 'anarchist solution', and if ever they find themselves departing from it they will still picture their new position in terms derived from it. Thus if they find themselves unable to countenance a full-blown picture of independent self-sufficient communes, they will still plump for severe forms of decentralization and devolution. Likewise they will only reluctantly accept the necessity for doing politics in the framework provided by the nation-state, and are much happier talking of 'acting locally and thinking globally', thus theorizing a by-pass of the nation-state and its most typical institutions.

In this sense, and bearing in mind the options presented to us by O'Riordan, the Green sustainable society can be negatively defined by saying that it will not be reached by transnational global cooperation, it will not principally be organized through the institutions of the nation-state, and it is not authoritarian (even though some of the earliest apologists associated with environmental politics, like Ophuls and Hardin, might give the impression that it is). Michael Allaby has said that, 'the environmental and self-sufficiency movements must make up their own minds whether they opt for the modified-anarchist or modified-fascist' (Allaby and Bunyard, 1980, p. 227). It seems to me quite clear that they have opted for the former, and that it would therefore be quite wrong to see ecologism as an ideology (like nationalism?) that can be either right or left wing. Understanding the political and intellectual nature of Green politics means seeing that its political prescriptions are fundamentally left-liberal, and if a text, a speech or an interview on the politics of the environment sounds different from that then it is not Green but something else.

So much (for now) for the political–institutional shape of the sustainable society, but what of the scientific and ethical practices that will be followed in it? Once again, Tim O'Riordan provides us with invaluable help by distinguishing between what he calls 'technocentrics' and 'ecocentrics'. Once again, both these positions start from the recognition that the 'natural' environment is being degraded at an unacceptable rate, but they adopt different postures with respect to what attitude consequently to strike. 'The technocentric ideology', writes O'Riordan, 'is almost arrogant in its assumption that man is supremely able to understand and control events to suit his purposes' (1981, p. 1). This is clearly in opposition to the message received by the Green movement from the *Limits to Growth* report that the complexity of the processes involved precisely prevents such understanding and control. In contrast, then, 'Ecocentrism preaches the virtues of reverence, humility, responsibility, and care; it argues for low-impact technology (but is not antitechnological); it decries bigness and impersonality in all its forms (but especially in the city); and demands a code of behaviour that seeks permanence and stability based upon ecological principles of diversity and homeostasis' (ibid.).

This is an admirable statement of the ethical and scientific centre of gravity of a Green sustainable society. Together with O'Riordan's political–institutional typology, it enables us to conclude that the general aspiration of Green ideologues, or the benchmark against which any picture of a sustainable society must be tested, is left–liberal ecocentrism. The expectations are for 'decentralization and local autonomy; a simpler, smaller-scale, face-to-face life closer to nature; labor-intensive modes of production; a deemphasis on material things; individual self-sufficiency . . .; and cultural diversity' (Ophuls, 1977, p. 164). This will provide the general rubric for the rest of the chapter, and now we are able to turn in more detail to the political and social principles of ecologism consequent upon the acceptance of the limits to growth thesis.

More problems with growth

'The notion that the living standards of the rich countries are attainable by all countries is pure fantasy', write Irvine and

Ponton (1988, p. 21), thus suggesting that there are physical limits to growth. As noted above, though, Greens also typically believe that there are social and ethical limits to growth. It has been argued, for example, by Green economists that indiscriminate growth exacerbates problems that it is intended to solve – particularly in the context of inflation and unemployment. It is suggested that unemployment is significantly the result of technological advances that reduce the labour/output ratio. The traditional idea that rates of unemployment can be brought down only by increased growth is challenged at two levels; first, that further growth and subsequent investment in the same direction (i.e. labour-saving technology) can result only in more unemployment not less; and second, that the rates of necessary growth projected by traditional political interests are unsustainable anyway. Either way unemployment in a growth-oriented economy at a British (or comparable) level of development is liable to structural increase, despite temporary fluctuations. The social costs of unemployment are unacceptable, say the Greens, and the aspiration of unlimited growth, being part of the problem, can hardly be a part of the solution.

At the same time Greens argue that the economics of growth are inherently inflationary. In the first place, and building on the position that scarcity is a fundamental and unavoidable datum on a finite planet, they suggest that as resources are depleted there will inevitably be upward pressure on prices. Similarly, the costs of economic growth (some of its 'externalities'), which have, up until now, been substantially ignored, will soon have to be taken into account and charged for. This, too, will increase the cost of living. Paul Ekins writes that 'environmental "goods" (e.g. clean air, pure water), which at a lower level of economic activity were effectively "free", will come to have an economic cost, resulting in further inflationary pressure' (1986, p. 11). This prophecy certainly seems to be coming true in Britain. It is widely accepted that our drinking water is unhealthy, substantially as a result of industrialized farming practices established in the context of the drive for growth, and costly measures are needed to clean it up. This will almost certainly contribute to inflationary pressure.

From a Green perspective, then, the problems of inflation and unemployment are (or will be) the products of growth and so cannot be solved by more of it. And the point above about the coming necessity of including the cost of cleaning up dirty water in economic projections also serves to illustrate Green concerns about traditional ways of measuring the strength of national economies. An increase, for example, in the Gross National Product (GNP) is invariably seen as a good thing, but, as Jonathon Porritt points out, 'Many of those goods and services [measured by GNP] are not beneficial to people: increased spending on crime, on pollution, on the many human casualties of our society; increased spending because of waste or planned obsolescence; increased spending because of growing bureaucracies' (1986, p. 121).

More particularly, Paul Ekins (1986, pp. 32–5) points to four reasons why Greens (and not a few others) consider GNP to be an inadequate measure of the health of an economy. First, it ignores the production that takes place in the non-monetarized part of the economy – such as household work, social work such as caring for the old and sick that takes place within the family, home-based production, and the myriad networks of production and exchange associated with the underground, or 'black', economy. The value of such informal production in some countries has been calculated at some 60 per cent of GNP (Ekins, 1986, p. 34). Second, GNP calculations give us no idea of the distribution of production or its fruits. Third, they give no indication, either, of the sustainability of the economic practices that contribute to production. For example, the American farming system generates huge profits (for some farmers) but is highly inefficient in terms of the ratio between the energy that is put into the system and the calorific value of the food it produces. Greens would question the wisdom of using economic indicators that pay no mind to the future viability of the system that they are measuring. Lastly, as pointed out above in the context of the clean water debate, GNP ignores the costs of production – particularly the environmental costs.

In the light of these criticisms, the fact that GNP is still the principal indicator of the health of national economies is, for Greens, symptomatic of the myopia induced by what they will see as an obsession with economic growth. In their view the success of a system of production and exchange can only really be judged once so-called 'defensive expenditures' have been removed from GNP calculations. Thus expenditure on environmental protection and on compensation for environmental damage, the costs of excessive urbanization and centralization (such as travel and trade costs), and the money spent on dealing with what Greens see as the problems brought about by 'industrial society' – all this should be removed from GNP calculations so as to give a measure of the quality of life as well as its quantity: 'progress in the future may consist in finding ways of reducing GNP', writes Jonathon Porritt (1986, p. 121).

It is in this last respect that the physical, social and ethical objections of the Greens to the economy and society of indiscriminate growth come together: such an economy and such a society are not very nice places in which to live. We are stunted ethically by the growth economy's refusal to take the quality of life of future generations seriously, and by its easy preparedness to take the Earth as resource rather than as blessing. We produce indiscriminately and consume voraciously and our status and aspirations are substantially judged and dictated by the wealth at our disposal. Greens believe that lives in the growth economy will tend away from the elegant and towards the grubby and materialistic. Conversely, they suggest that a society orientated around sustainable growth would be a less greedy and more pleasant place in which to live, and I shall be covering some of the arguments in favour of this position as the chapter progresses. For the moment, as a temporary bulwark against disbelief, Greens might quote John Stuart Mill in their favour:

It is scarcely necessary to remark that a stationary condition of capital and population implies no stationary state of human improvement. There would be as much scope as ever for all kinds of mental culture, and moral and social progress; as much room for improving the Art of Living and much more likelihood of its being improved. (quoted in Meadows *et al.*, 1983, p. 175)

Questioning consumption

Political ecologists argue, then, for a contraction in economic growth. In the terms set out by Herman Daly this involves a contraction in the various components of what he calls 'throughput' (in Ekins, 1986, p. 13) – the components being resource depletion, production, consumption and waste. Of these four, it is probably production that receives most attention when commentators consider the bases and implications of the sustainable society, but it seems to me that consumption provides the most useful starting-point for discussion. In the first place this is because the other three terms are founded upon the existence and persistence of consumption: consumption implies depletion implies production implies waste. And secondly, the picture of the Good Life that the political ideology of ecologism paints for us is differentiated from most other pictures precisely because of its arguing for less consumption. Not only does this mark off ecologism from most other political ideologies but it also helps to distinguish it from light-green environmentalism. Jonathon Porritt, for example, writes in dark-green rather than light-green mode when he says that 'A low-energy strategy means a low-consumption economy; we can do more with less, but we'd be better off doing less with less' (1986, p. 174). In this context, to concentrate on consumption and its implications is both to help mark out ecologism's proper territory and to keep in mind that in this respect at least it comprises 'a sharp break with the principles of the modern era' (Ophuls, 1977, p. 164).

[89]

As with growth, the Green questioning of consumption has both a pragmatic and an elegiac content. Irvine and Ponton suggest that 'an attitude of "enough" must replace that of "more" ' (1988, p. 15), and Porritt, likewise, argues that, 'It's time for the economics of enough' (1986, p. 125), not only because they feel that present rates of consumption are physically unsustainable but also because they are unseemly. They balk at the production and purchase of what they consider to be unnecessary items, and press for a life based on 'voluntary simplicity' (ibid., p. 204). The 'middle way between indulgence and poverty' (ibid.), which would be the way of the sustainable society, might be uncomfortable for some: 'Of course people will still have washing-machines (as long as they are energy-efficient). But electric toothbrushes and carving-knives? That's another matter!' (Bunyard and Morgan-Grenville, 1987, p. 335).

Essential, then, to ecologism's picture of the sustainable society is reduced consumption (in profligate 'advanced' industrial countries, at any rate), and equally essential is the idea that, while this might involve a reduced material standard of living, such sacrifice will be more than made up for by the benefits to be gained. Greens will always distinguish between quantity and quality: 'in terms of crude material wealth, we're not likely to get any wealthier. But . . . what matters now is the quality of wealth' (Porritt, 1986, p. 124). In similar vein Edward Goldsmith reckons that the specious satisfactions of consumption can and should be replaced by 'Satisfactions of a non-material kind . . . social ones' (1988, pp. 197–8), and for Bunyard and Morgan-Grenville (or one of their contributors) the sky is the limit:

Judged by illusory standards of wealth we might well be 'poorer' in a Green future – but we would, *in reality*, have a higher standard of living, better food, healthier bodies, rewarding work, good companionship, cleaner air, greater self-reliance, more supportive communities and, above all, a safer world to live in. (1987, p. 335)

Given the centrality of reduced consumption to the Green project, for all the reasons given above, it is surprising that so few of ecologism's theorists (as far as I am aware) have paid much serious attention to the role of advertising in reproducing the habits and practices of consumption that they seek to criticize. Irvine and Ponton prove themselves exceptions to this general rule in pointing out that 'Linking mass production and mass consumption is the advertising industry' (1988, p. 62). It seems to me that in this respect there may be a political strategy lurking in marketing's murky entrails – exposure of the social irresponsibility (from the point of view of sustainability) of the advertising industry would be a concrete way of raising the issue of consumption (well beyond, and in opposition to, the phenomenon of green consumerism) and making clearer what a sustainable society might look like. As Irvine and Ponton go on to say: 'Notions such as durability, reduced or shared consumption, or substituting non-material pleasures for the use of objects, conflict with the requirements of mass marketing. Advertising is tied to an expanding economy, the one thing that we, living on a finite planet, must avoid' (ibid., p. 63). In this sense, basic *nostra* of the Green movement come together in the same place: the finitude of the planet, the need to restrict growth, the consequent need to reduce consumption, and the necessity for calling into question the practices (in this case advertising) that help reproduce the growth economy.

Questioning consumption: need

Reducing material consumption is an integral part of ecologism's project and so the Green movement has a profound political and intellectual problem on its hands. It is faced, in the first place, with persuading potential supporters that this is a desirable aspiration, and it is saddled with a series of intellectual arguments for its position that presently appear too weak to do the job required. The assertion, noted above, that a society organized around reduced consumption just *would* be more pleasurable to live in seems unlikely – in present circumstances

[91]

– to cut the necessary ice. Likewise, the most favoured alternative strategy, the building of a theory of need, is notoriously difficult to carry out. How did Bunyard and Morgan-Grenville, above, arrive at the conclusion that washing-machines are legitimate objects but that electric toothbrushes are not? There is evidently a theory (or more likely an intuition) of need at work here, but how is it to be persuasively expressed? Paul Ekins, for one, thinks that it is important for the Green movement to answer this query – 'The question of human needs is of absolutely central significance to the New Economics' (1986, p. 55) – but most expressions of theories of need are far too vague to be of much use: 'needs being those things that are essential to our survival and to civilized human existence, wants being the extras that serve to satisfy our desires' (Porritt, 1986, p. 196).

The problem with such a formulation is that, while it gives us an idea of the general differences between needs and wants, it does not help us concretely to fill out their content. At the same time, to be able to fill out their content in any universal sense presupposes that 'fundamental human needs are finite, few and classifiable' (Ekins, 1986, p. 49). The obvious objection to this – that needs are historically and culturally mediated – can be partly met by saying that 'fundamental human needs are the same in all cultures and all historical periods. What changes, both over time and through cultures, is the form or the means by which these needs are satisfied' (ibid.). In this way a distinction is created between 'needs' and 'satisfiers' – the needs are permanent and the satisfiers are contingent and therefore open to negotiation.

But how far does this help? – the distinction just pushes the problem back one place. We might all be able to agree on certain 'basic needs' (food, drink, clothing, shelter), but the 'satisfiers' are another matter, and they are precisely what have to be negotiated. As Jonathon Porritt remarks, 'We all need to get from A to B; some people insist they can manage such a feat only in the back of a Rolls Royce' (1986, p. 196). Just what size car is acceptable? Is a car acceptable at all?

If the needs/wants problem seems presently intractable, it is enough to notice for our purposes – that of identifying the principal aspects of the Green sustainable society – that the emphasis on reduced consumption brings up the question sooner or later, and that therefore the distinction between needs and wants is one of the intellectual features of the various pictures of such a society. At the same time, the sense of scarcity that informs the whole discussion also generates another characteristic of the sustainable society to which most of its supporters will subscribe: a tendency towards the egalitarian distribution of the material wealth that is available. Thus Porritt suggests that 'redistribution is a precondition for any transition to a stable society', and, more fully, Irvine and Ponton explain that, 'If there are limits to the needs for which society can provide, their fair distribution is even more urgent . . . Limiting differentials between people is as essential as limiting economic growth and technological innovation' (1988, p. 80). In this respect the sustainable society of Green politics approximates closely to socialistic conceptions of equality in calling for reduced differentials, although it is clear in other respects that the stress on equality of opportunity means that there will be room for differentials, 'fairly' arrived at.

Questioning consumption: population

So we can identify a Green belief in the benefits and necessity of reducing levels of material consumption, and the problems associated with convincing enough of us (for it to make any appreciable difference) to do so. But Greens have another way of reducing consumption – one that does not involve intricate argumentation. Porritt is most clear in this respect: 'In terms of reducing overall consumption, there's nothing more effective than reducing the number of people doing the consuming' (1986, p. 190). Greens are aware that some people in some countries consume much more than other people in other countries, and that therefore it is far too simplistic to argue for across-the-board reductions: 'Per capita energy consumption in the United States is two and one-half times the European average and thousands of times that of many Third World countries' (Tokar, 1987, p. 72). Nevertheless, the option of population reduction is rather more contentious than it is elegant, constituting as it does a specific aspect of the general Green position that even present population levels are unsustainable, let alone projected future levels. Experience suggests that this message is a difficult one to swallow for very many people.

The *British Green Party Manifesto* of 1987 stated delicately that 'The Green Party is convinced that an important aspect of lightening our impact on the land is to reduce our own numbers' (1987, p. 11), while others are somewhat more direct and dramatic: 'The explosion in human numbers is the greatest long-term threat to the future of human and non-human inhabitants of the Earth' (Irvine and Ponton, 1988, p. 17). It is certainly central to all Green pictures of the sustainable society that population levels would be lower than they presently are, although there is disagreement about what levels actually would be sustainable. Irvine and Ponton put the level for Britain at about 30 million people, which is (as they say) about half its present level (ibid., p. 22), and is in line with the British Green Party's estimate as set out in its *Manifesto for a Sustainable Society*. Bunyard and Morgan-Grenville, however, suggest that Britain could sustain 55 million people more or less self-reliantly – but only if we could all first be converted to vegetarianism (1987, pp. 94–6). Edward Goldsmith has put the globally sustainable figure at 3,500 million ('and probably a good deal less' – 1972, p. 57), which means somehow losing about 1,500 million of the present world population.

And of course this is exactly the problem: how to 'lose' 1,500 million people. In the furthest reaches of some groups associated with the Green movement, draconian measures for solving this problem have been advanced. As reported in Chapter 2, the Earth First! group in the United States of America has suggested that epidemics such as AIDS should be allowed to run their course so as to help rid us of excess population. These are the sorts of pronouncements that have hampered the Green movement's attempts to get its population policies taken seriously; indeed, there appears to be a sense in which the mere mention of population control brings to the minds of well-intentioned people the unacceptable images associated with seal-culling, and the subsequent suggestion that this is not for human beings.

At the same time, the left has been fighting a running battle with Malthus and his supporters ever since 1792 and the publication of the *Essay on the Principle of Population*, and they will generally respond to the Green position by arguing that starvation is caused primarily by uneven distribution of resources rather than by their absolute limitation. Greens have substantially accepted this response, but in the same way in which they will point to the absolute limits on resource extraction despite temporary respites gained by our ingenuity in extracting them, they will also suggest that there just are limits to the population that can be sustainably and comfortably maintained on a finite planet.

Despite the contributions of groups such as Earth First!, Greens usually suggest that population control and reduction, although considered absolutely necessary, are a matter for negotiation rather than imposition. Thus the British Green Party rejects 'unpalatable legislation' (*Manifesto*, 1987, p. 11) and Arne Naess in his Schumacher lecture of 1987 recognized that reaching a sustainable population might take hundreds of years – this because 'It remains vitally important to reject coercive measures as an unacceptable and morally repugnant infringement of human rights' (Porritt, 1986, p. 193). The kinds of tactic that have therefore been suggested within the Green movement are summed up by Irvine and Ponton:

> There could be payments for periods of non-pregnancy and non-birth (a kind of no claims bonus); tax benefits for families with fewer than two children; sterilization bonuses; withdrawal of maternity and similar benefits after a second child; larger pensions for people with fewer than two children; free, easily

[95]

available family planning; more funds for research into means of contraception, especially for men; an end to fertility research and treatment; a more realistic approach to abortion; the banning of surrogate motherhood and similar practices; and the promotion of equal opportunities for women in all areas of life. (1988, p. 23).

With respect to the last point the authors stress that 'There is a happy correlation between women's liberation and population control' (ibid.), and as for the rest, while it is clear that there are sticks as well as carrots at work (and that measures such as sterilization bonuses have often proved unwieldy, offensive and open to abuse), such tactics are a far cry from the culling feared by the Greens' opponents and recommended by some deep ecologists.

However, it would be wrong so easily to absolve Green strategy with respect to population control from any potential connection with repression. It has been suggested by some of the movement's supporters that communities (whether nation-states or some other political–institutional formation) will need to be protected from population growth by some form of immigration control. This was most notoriously suggested by Garrett Hardin in the wake of his development of the lifeboat ethic, which had it that if there was enough room for only ten people to survive in a lifeboat then the eleventh (generally read as Third World populations) would have to be thrown out. This is not standard fare in the Green movement today, but it has its echoes, I suggest, in some remarks about immigration control.

Jonathon Porritt, for example, announces that 'The strictly logical position, as far as ecologists are concerned, is to keep immigration at the lowest possible level while remaining sensitive to the needs of refugees, split families, political exiles etc.' (1986, p. 191), and Edward Goldsmith recommends that 'a community must be relatively closed' (1988, p. 203). The repressive tribalism and exclusion that this could generate is absolutely clear in Goldsmith:

[96]

a certain number of 'foreigners' could be allowed to settle but
again . . . they would not, thereby, partake in the running of
the community until such time as the citizens elected them to be
of their number. (ibid.)

Rather like the background radiation that gives us evidence
of the Big Bang, these strictures on immigration are the
vestigial remnants of shocking discoveries and violent
solutions. The Green movement would do well, I think, to
abandon them altogether, for they serve little purpose today.
They even help to make a nonsense of some other Green
positions, such as that 'Greens celebrate the diversity of culture
in a multi-cultural society', and that 'our goal is equality of
opportunity for members of all ethnic communities' (*Manifesto*,
1987, pp. 14–15). It is hard to see how Porritt could have his
way of keeping immigration at the lowest possible level and at
the same time argue that this should be '*in no way* discriminatory
in terms of race or colour' (1986, p. 191). Immigration controls
just do discriminate in terms of race or colour (or in terms of
difference, generally) and Green politics has, I believe, no need
for them. In the first place, the numbers concerned are tiny, and
in the second place the issue of immigration obscures the real
and pressing problem (for the Greens), which is that of
stabilizing and then reducing the exploding world population.

Questioning consumption: technology

Pretty soon, discussion of the Green sustainable society raises
the issue of the role and place of technology. To the extent that
Green politics is a challenge to the norms and practices of late
twentieth-century science and society, and to the extent that it
will blame scientific development (in a certain direction) for
many of the ills it conceives we now suffer, and to the extent,
finally, that it attacks the belief that more of the same will cure
those ills, technology is always under the critical Green
microscope. It is this, of course, that has led those outside the
movement (and not a few, it has to be said, within it) to view

it as anti-technological and therefore (a *non sequitur*) as a call to return to a pre-technological age.

This is far too simplistic. The most that can be said, I have concluded, about the Green movement's attitude to nineteenth- and twentieth-century technology (which is what I will substantially mean by 'technology' from now on) is that it is ambivalent and that, more specifically, it depends what kind of technology you are talking about. Rudolf Bahro of Germany, for instance, is pretty much against most forms of technology; Jonathon Porritt is in favour of certain sorts, but generally likes to remain agnostic; and Brian Tokar, of the USA, is suspicious of it. What can be said, it seems to me, is that wholehearted acceptance of any form of technology disqualifies one from membership of the Green canon; thus André Gorz and Alvin Toffler, for instance, in substantially basing their Utopias on technology, do not adopt Green stances towards it. Put differently, although much attention has been focused on Green attitudes to technology, Greens are likely to want the spotlight turned elsewhere: more specifically, towards the moral and spiritual changes that they conceive to be necessary for the practice of sustainable societies. We should remember that Greens are forever suspicious of the 'technological fix', and to this extent suspicion towards technology in general is a fundamental feature of the Green intellectual make-up.

We can see how this works for the Greens by their distinguishing between what Edward Goldsmith calls the 'real world' and the 'surrogate world' – the former comprising things like trees and topsoil, and the latter being the world that we make or fashion (1988, pp. 185 ff). Greens will most usually gravitate towards what they conceive to be the authenticity of the 'real world' and would probably like to have it stay substantially as it is. They know that this cannot be, but will want changes to it convincingly justified. In this context the apparently mundane Community Ground Rent proposed by the British Green Party, according to which 'the nearer the land is to its natural state, the lower the Community Ground Rent will be' (*Manifesto*, 1987, p. 7), takes on the guise of an expression of one of the most profound aspects of Green motivation: the privileging of the real world against the surrogate one. Green attitudes to technology must be seen in this context, and Allaby and Bunyard have captured the picture well: 'to the environmentalist nuclear power is almost certain to be unacceptable, overseas travel by jet aircraft is likely to raise moral qualms, and microprocessors are viewed with a distinct feeling of unease' (1980, p. 63).

This ambivalence can be instructively expressed by referring to the issue of recycling. Evidently the technology exists to recycle large amounts of 'waste' material (newspapers, bottles, etc.) and make it useful again. This is probably the kind of activity most often associated with Green politics, and it is true that members of the Green movement will often base their pictures of the sustainable society on such strategies: 'We have already suggested that the key to pollution control is not dispersal but recycling' (Goldsmith, 1972, p. 43), and, 'Our policies on resources would reduce . . . waste by encouraging policies of re-use and recycling' (*Manifesto*, 1987, p. 19).

In the wider context of the Green demand for reduced consumption, however, this is clearly not enough, and some Greens will be worried that excessive reliance on recycling will shift the onus away from the recognition that more profound changes are required. The emphasis should be on reducing consumption rather than recycling that which has already been consumed. Thus, in a formulation to which I have already referred:

> The fiction of combining present levels of consumption with 'limitless recycling' is more characteristic of the technocratic vision than of an ecological one. Recycling itself uses resources, expends energy, creates thermal pollution; on the bottom line, it's just an industrial activity like all the others. Recycling is both useful and necessary – but it is an illusion to imagine that it provides any basic answers. (Porritt, 1986, p. 183)

Greens will insist that in this connection Porritt's basic answers can be provided only by 'A reduction in the total amount of resources we are consuming' (Irvine and Ponton, 1988, p. 28), and by answering the following questions (and particularly the second) from Brian Tokar in the affirmative: 'If something cannot be manufactured, built or grown without causing irreparable ecological damage, can't we strive to create something to take its place, or simply decide to do without it?' (1987, pp. 73–4). The option of doing without things (which is not, interestingly, mentioned in the British Green Party's 1987 manifesto) is a direct result of Greens demanding reduced consumption – a demand that consistently recognizes that even appropriate use of technology is a holding operation rather than an assault on the principal issues.

While there is some ambivalence over the Green attitude to technology's capability of dealing with the problem of limited resources, there is even more disagreement over its general role in the sustainable society. We might wonder, for instance, what kinds of technology will be allowed in order to cope with the demands of defending Green societies from potential or actual aggressors. Some Green thinkers will sidestep the issue, of course, by arguing that sustainable societies will be basically peaceful ones anyway. Others will advocate non-violent civil resistance, drawing on practices followed, for example, during the 1980s' anti-nuclear actions and demonstrations. This is fine as long as one is not fired upon, or is prepared to die defenceless if one is.

But most Green scenarios for defence involve some variation of the 'hedgehog principle' – that the attacked population makes itself as prickly and uncomfortable for the invading forces as possible: 'A high enough level of non-cooperation, civil disobedience and sabotage', suggests Brian Tokar, 'should be sufficient to make any country ungovernable' (1987, p. 121). This may be true, but civil disobedience and sabotage in the face of an aggressor willing to use force, if they are not to be enormously wasteful of human life, can make high technology demands. How far would a Green society be prepared to go along the road of weapons technology and its associated spin-offs?

Again it has been suggested more positively that, far from being a *bête noire*, technology can make more palatable the transition to, and practice of, more localized and frugal forms of living. One of the major fears of observers outside the Green movement is that its picture of localized politics smacks of a petty parochialism, which would be both undesirable and unpleasant to live with. But would not information technology reduce the likelihood of this? Is this not precisely the sort of thing that Edward Goldsmith was thinking of when he wrote of 'the technological infrastructure of a decentralised society' (Goldsmith, 1972, p. 86)?

Greens will often be heard contending that one of the beauties of modern technology is that is is ideally suited to decentralized forms of politics, and the vision of the computer terminal in every home is just one expression of this. Jonathon Porritt, for one, appears enthusiastic about the possibilities as he advocates 'smaller, more self-reliant communities': 'with modern communications technology, there need be no fear of a return to the mean-minded parochialism of pre-industrial Britain' (1986, p. 166). Such a view is more generally supported by the British Green Party:

> We favour appropriate technology: technology that is good and satisfying to work with, produces useful end results, and is kind to the environment. Many such technologies will be 'high-tech'. (*Manifesto*, 1987, p. 4)

In this respect we would seem entitled to agree with William Ophuls when he contends that 'The picture of the frugal society that thus emerges resembles something like the city-state form of civilization, but on a much higher and more sophisticated technological base' (1977, p. 168).

However, it would be wrong to leave Green thoughts on the general role of technology in the sustainable society at this Toffleresque level. Just as Porritt worries about the resource use and waste associated with recycling technology, so others in the movement worry about the environmental implications of his information technology society: many of the processes involved in microchip production, for example, are anything but environmentally benign. Brian Tokar observes that 'electronics manufacture, underneath its clean facade, is a series of dangerous chemical processes' (1987, pp. 76–7), and these processes involve the creation of more and more compounds of which the 'natural' world has no evolutionary experience, so reducing the likelihood of their being safely broken down. Tokar continues: 'The "information society" does not use any fewer goods; it simply seeks to better hide the consequences of their production' (ibid., p. 77). In this respect, some Greens will always adopt an attitude of suspicion towards the so-called surrogate world.

Energy

If reduced consumption rather than more technological devices is the answer to the problems raised by the absolute scarcity of resources, then Greens will point out that the same must apply to the use of energy. Energy is, of course, a resource and, to the extent that present global energy policies rely principally on non-renewable sources of energy, it is also a limited resource. Nuclear power itself is produced from the limited resource of uranium and so, unless recent reports of nuclear fusion in a test-tube prove to have some foundation, the nuclear option evidently cannot solve the problems brought about by resource scarcity. At the same time, while actual resource levels might be quite high, *available* non-renewable energy resource levels will be somewhat lower. This is because, in the first place, the cost of extraction (it is argued by the Greens) will eventually reach unacceptable heights; and second, there must come a point where, as Herman Daly puts it, it will cost as much energy 'to mine a ton of coal as can be got from a ton of coal' (1977b, p. 111).

Beyond the problem of the limits of non-renewable energy resources, Greens are also typically wary of the use of such resources for the environmental damage they can cause. Nuclear energy is potentially highly polluting, the problems of disposing of even low-level waste (often referred to as the nuclear industry's 'Achilles heel') have not been satisfactorily solved, and nuclear power stations under normal operating circumstances might just be a source of leukemia. Likewise, fossil-fuel power stations notoriously contribute to the greenhouse effect and are one of the causes of acid rain. Technological mollification of these latter problems is possible: 'Strict pollution controls would reduce the environmental effects of burning hydrocarbons to less than 20 per cent of their present level' (Bunyard and Morgan-Grenville, 1987, p. 158), but such strategies are subject to the same kind of criticism advanced by Jonathon Porritt in connection with recycling, above.

In the face of the perceived disadvantages of relying for energy on limited stocks of polluting and dangerous non-renewable resources, Greens usually base their energy strategy around renewable sources of energy, conservation of energy – 'The most important energy source of all is conservation' (Porritt, 1986, p. 175) – and reduced consumption, of both energy and the durable objects that it helps us produce. Renewable energy sources are argued to be desirable because they are in principle unlimited, they are relatively environmentally benign, and they are suited to the decentralized forms of living most often recommended by political ecologists. In all these respects they speak to the basic demands of the Green sustainable society. It is worth remarking, however, that in one respect they do not. The technology associated with renewable energy sources (windmills, barrages) is often highly complex and, in the case of the production of solar cells, polluting. Remembering the objections to the technologies associated with recycling and information technology, we can see that the issue of alternative energy sources provides us with yet another specific example of the ambivalence with which Greens will view the role of technology.

Few Greens pretend, however, that the energy policy referred to above will produce the fantastic quantities of energy presently required, let alone cope with the dizzying projections associated with the developing nations: 'Dreams of powering the current lifestyles of the industrialized countries from alternative energy sources are illusory' (Irvine and Ponton, 1988, p. 53). This means that demand for energy will have to lessen beyond the reductions brought about by price increases and improved conservation policies. At this point, the Green assertion that sustainability will involve reducing material consumption meets the energy problem. Reduced energy use, for the Green movement, involves reduced production, and reduced production involves reduced consumption. The point is that 'we can satisfy our needs today from these sources [wind, water, sun] without robbing future generations of their energy supply' (ibid., p. 55), but we cannot satisfy what Greens would regard as our greed. Once again, the distinction between needs and wants is raised, and once again we see that the Green picture of the sustainable society is buttressed by the necessity and desirability of reduced material consumption.

Trade and travel

Consistent with the principles of self-reliance and communitarian decentralization that inform the sustainable society, Greens have unfashionable views on the issues of trade and travel. Before discussing this in a little detail it is important to be clear that self-reliance is not the same as self-sufficiency and that Greens go to some lengths to distinguish the two. Despite Green politics often being identified with the self-sufficiency commune movement (quite properly, in a sense, given that many of its members practise such self-sufficiency and that some of its major theorists – e.g. Rudolf Bahro – come very close to envisaging Green societies in this way), my understanding is that Green politics is most generally seen to be organized around principles of self-reliance rather than self-sufficiency.

What is the difference? Self-sufficiency can be described as 'a state of absolute economic independence', while self-reliance is best understood as 'a state of relative independence' (Bunyard and Morgan-Grenville, 1987, p. 334). In terms of the importance of the notion of self-reliance to the politics of ecology, Paul Ekins goes so far as to report that, along with theories of need (already covered) and a reconceptualization of work (see below), it is one of the three pillars of the New Economic framework (1987, p. 97). According to Johan Galtung, the basic rules that the theory of self-reliance gives rise to are:

> produce what you need using your own resources, internalising the challenge this involves, growing with the challenges, neither giving the most challenging tasks (positive externalities) to somebody else on whom you become dependent, nor exporting negative externalities to somebody else to whom you do damage and who may become dependent on you. (in Ekins, 1986, p. 101)

On this reading, trade is something to be carried out as an exception rather than as a rule. There is nothing in the theory of self-reliance that forbids trade, but it certainly aims to shift the onus of justification away from those who would reduce it and on to those who would maximize it. It would be wrong, then, to characterize Greens as recommending complete economic independence – they are perfectly aware that 'There are always goods or services that cannot be generated or provided locally, regionally or nationally' (ibid., p. 52). The ground-rule, however, would be that 'self-reliance starts with the idea of producing things yourself rather than getting them through exchange' (ibid., p. 104). Imagining this rule being followed amounts to imagining an important part of the economic and political framework within which a Green sustainable society would operate.

Trade is viewed with suspicion by Greens on four grounds. In the first place (not necessarily a Green reason) it is a site of the exercise of political and economic power and an easy way to exchange self-determination for dependence; second, it encourages frippery and helps to turn wants into needs (do we need kiwi fruits? – but, then, do we need tea?); third, patterns of trade end up being notiously wasteful of resources, as tomatoes (for example) are grown on the island of Guernsey, exported, and then sometimes shipped back for consumption; and fourth, reliance on one or two products for export can render economies vulnerable to a drop in prices or a general worsening of the terms of trade.

It is this last point that leads Johan Galtung to suggest that, if trade is to take place, 'one field of production – production for basic needs [food, clothing, shelter, energy, health, education, home defence] – should be carried out in such a way that the country is at least potentially self-sufficient, not only self-reliant' (ibid., p. 102). In this way populations would be shielded, at least in terms of necessities, from the vagaries of the market. As a result of these views on trade, Green economic practice would be built substantially around protectionism: 'it's clear that selective protection of the domestic economy will be needed to establish its sustainable basis, and to encourage the country to become far more self-sufficient than it is at present' (Porritt, 1986, p. 135).

Understanding this will help us to understand why much-vaunted 'green' politicians such as Norway's Prime Minister Gro Harlem Brundtland have a long way to go before embracing the Green programme as such. In this context she argues that, 'protectionism is one of the aspects of confrontation [between nations] which needs to be abolished . . . The advantages of free trade for the countries of the North and South ought to be evident' (1989, p. 5). In the present political climate this is standard fare, and provides a further illustration of the way in which political ecology sets its face against dominant paradigms.

Likewise, supporting the Green argument for reduced trade we find the central notions of reduced consumption (if you can't produce it, think about doing without it first, and only trading for it second), and a theory of need that hopes to sustain the view that in many instances the trade to which we have become accustomed is an unwarranted indulgence. If life under these circumstances sounds like reproducing the styles of life most often associated with Third World countries, then the Green position on trade (and not a few of their other recommendations) reflects Rudolf Bahro's view that, 'With a pinch of salt one might say . . . the path of reconciliation with the Third World might consist in our becoming Third World ourselves' (1986, p. 88).

Part of the effect of protectionism, of course, would be to throw communities back on to their own resources, and this is entirely in line with the Green plan of creating a political life founded upon communitarian decentralization. This plan also affects the Green position on travel: one of the characteristics of the Green sustainable society is that people would travel less. Arne Naess in his 1987 Schumacher lecture referred to the principle of 'limited mobility' and William Ophuls, too, believes that personal mobility would be limited in such a society (1977, p. 167). In the first place this is because Greens consider present travel practices to be wasteful of resources – Rudolf Bahro, especially, is particularly difficult to coax onto an aeroplane for this reason.

Secondly, and more importantly, Greens argue for reduced mobility as a part of their hopes for generating supportive, satisfying relationships in their decentralized, self-reliant communities. From this point of view, travel involves dislocation of the ties that hold such communities together, and so endangers the emergence of the 'sense of loyalty and involvement' (Porritt, 1986, p. 166) that, for Greens, will be one of the prime benefits of decentralized communitarian life. The sustainable society is substantially about living 'in place' and developing an intimacy with it and the people who live there; travel, on this reading, is too expansive and too centrifugal an occupation.

Work

Paul Ekins refers to 'a reconceptualisation of the nature and value of work' as one of the principal pillars of the Green economic and social framework (1986, p. 97), and it is certainly true that ecologism can be marked off from most other modern political ideologies by its attitude to the subject. Political ecologists have a specific view on the value of work and they also question the dominant tendency to associate work with paid employment. Such an association can lead us to believe that if a person is not in paid employment then they are not working. This, for Greens is simply untrue, and their renegotiation of the meaning of work leads them to suggest ways of 'freeing' it from what they see as restrictions founded on the modern (and archaic) sense that work just is paid employment. This will become clearer shortly, but first a word needs to be said about how Greens typically value work itself.

One of the most common scenarios for advanced industrial societies in this context is the workless future. This is a familiar story – one that begins in automated car factories and suggests that technological advances will eventually enable us to enjoy more or less labourless production across vast swathes of the industrial process. In this future the only problem would be how best to use the increased leisure time created by clean and automated production. Greens have peered into this future and they do not like what they see.

In the first place they will claim that it pays no mind whatever to the problems of sustainability on a finite planet. Then, to the extent that that future is already with us, political ecologists will object to the unemployment that automated production appears to cause, and they typically reject claims that other industries (service, 'sunrise') will take up the employment slack caused by industrial reconversion. Third, such a future (given the present general antipathy to redistribution) would most likely produce a society split between the highly paid monitors of machinery and the stunted recipients of social security payments pitched at a level designed to discourage indolence. Finally, Greens look at the burgeoning leisure industry and see its consumer-oriented, environmentally damaging, industrialized and disciplined nature as a threat to the self-reliant, productive practices that the Green Good Life holds out for us.

But beyond even all this, Greens will (at the very least) be sceptical of the workless future because they think work is a good thing to do. In this respect they insert themselves in the tradition that has it that work is a noble occupation; that it uplifts the spirit and helps create and reproduce ties with one's community – even helps to create oneself. This view has it that work is an obligation both to oneself and to one's society, and that this obligation has to be redeemed. Thus Jonathon Porritt, for example, states: 'I must confess to being revolutionary in a very old-fashioned way when it comes to work. The statement of Thomas Aquinas, "There can be no joy of life without the joy of work", just about sums it up for me'. He continues: 'I'm one of those who consider work to be a necessity of the human condition, a defining characteristic of the sort of people we are'; and finally, 'Far from universal automation "solving our economic problems", I believe it would so impair our humanity as to make life utterly meaningless' (1986, p. 127).

This is evidently another respect in which Green politics clearly confronts the dominant post-industrial vision. Automated production is precisely one of the features of that vision and while Porritt (at least) hedges his bets just a little – 'One undisputed advantage of microprocessors is that they will enable machines to do jobs that are boring, unhealthy, unpleasant and dangerous' (ibid., p. 129) – the general understanding of the Green position is that it advocates that the emphasis be in principle on labour-intensive production. It should be noted that, in the wider context of the Green sustainable society and the reasons for its necessity (limits to growth), this is not simply because work is a fulfilling thing to do, but because it will become a standard requirement: 'With more people and fewer resources, the capital/labour ratio must start shifting back towards labour-intensive production' (ibid.). In other words, as the price of resources goes up (as Greens believe it will do, in the context of scarcity), the amount of capital available for reinvestment in labour-saving machinery will go down. This, it is held, will swing the balance back in favour of more labour-intensive production. For all these reasons, then, the Green sustainable society will be more labour-intensive than the one we presently occupy.

The Green favouring of work will evidently lead political ecologists – like most other people – to bemoan the existence of unemployment, but Greens add a twist to the expected story. They will claim that, while there is clearly unemployment, that does not mean that there is no work being done. At the root of this judgement lies the belief that work should not be seen as synonymous with paid employment. Greens (and, once again, not a few others) point out that enormous amounts of work are done that do not register as work, precisely because the tasks do not take the form of paid employment. Examples of this would be work done by women (mainly) in the home, caring for the sick and elderly outside the institutions of care, and work done in the so-called 'informal' economy.

Greens point out that this distinction is not merely of semantic importance. The modern tendency of associating reward and status with paid employment results in employers and potential employees looking to the sectors of production traditionally associated with paid employment when it comes to strategies for dealing with unemployment. In other words, the unemployed look for work in paid employment and employers try to place them in such employment. The Green approach to problems of unemployment, in contrast, is to concentrate on those areas where work has always been done, but where it is frowned upon – if not actually criminalized. Nothing, evidently, is solved by semantically collapsing the distinction between work and paid employment, but Greens argue for a series of policies that would practise such a collapse.

Most generally, the Green argument is prefaced by the belief that traditional solutions to the problems of unemployment (like more growth) are doomed to failure either because of the context of a finite planet, or because the technological infrastructure that has been built up is actually designed to reduce places of paid employment. Irvine and Ponton are clear about the implications: 'In these circumstances slogans about "No Return to the 30's" and "Jobs for All" are irrelevant if not downright reactionary' (1988, pp. 66–7). Political ecologists will go on from here to say that the work that is done in the informal economy must be liberated and de-criminalized, and that policies presently designed to prevent people from working in the informal economy should be abandoned and replaced by policies that will encourage them to work there. In this sense, collapsing the distinction between work and paid employment means collapsing the distinction between the formal and the informal economy.

The reasons Greens give for why the potential of the informal economy is presently not fully realized revolve around the role played by current systems of social security and the assumptions that inform them. Greens point out that most social security systems deter people from doing work on a part-time, irregular basis (i.e. just when it 'shows up') because benefits are likely to be withdrawn – in other words, it is not always financially worthwhile to work. Second, rises in income can also lead to the withdrawal of benefits, leading to what has been called the 'poverty trap' (*Manifesto*, 1987, p. 6). For these two reasons, work in the informal economy, the conditions of which bear little relation to the rigid structures of paid employment, is effectively discouraged. Furthermore, most social security systems (and certainly Britain's, based on Beveridge's 1942 proposal) have been designed around the assumptions of a growth economy and a system of reward based on the existence of practically universal paid employment. Once those assumptions no longer hold (and Greens believe that they do not), the social security system based upon them must come into question too.

Beyond these points, Greens are typically critical of the means-testing that is part and parcel of current social security strategies and, associated with this, they are offended by the conditionality of awards and the repercussions this has: 'There are far more unclaimed benefits than illegal claims, though we have not seen many teams of investigators seeking out non-claimants' (Irvine and Ponton, 1988, p. 84). The solution most often canvassed in Green literature to the problems associated with present social security systems and, particularly, the way in which they help marginalize the informal economy, is a minimum income (MIS) or guaranteed basic income scheme (GBIS).

The general form of the GBIS is simply expressed. According to the *British Green Party Manifesto* it would provide:

> an automatic weekly payment to everybody throughout life, regardless of sex or marital status, non-means tested and tax free, at different rates for different age-groups. Children's payments would go to the mother or whoever has legal responsibility of the care of the child. (1987, p. 5)

Likewise, Anne Miller reports that:

> A Basic Income Scheme would aim to guarantee each man, woman and child the unconditional right to an independent income sufficient to meet basic living costs. Its main purpose would be the prevention of poverty, as opposed to mere poverty relief. (in Ekins, 1986, p. 226)

Advocates of the GBIS claim that it has distinct advantages with respect to the drawbacks and anomalies of standard social security systems. First, people will not be discouraged from taking part-time, irregular work, because no drop in benefit will be involved; second, small rises in income will not affect benefit payments either; and third, the system would be much simpler to administer than most present ones. More generally, flexible working patterns would be encouraged, leading (it is hoped) to the liberation of the informal economy and its recognition as a site of respectable employment. At the same time, Greens hope that the GBIS would help to break down what they consider to be an insidious distinction in status between those employed and those unemployed.

Ever since their inception (and the Greens are not the only ones to have argued for guaranteed basic income schemes – Milton Friedman has been associated with them too, for example) such schemes have been highly controversial. In the first place, people ask how much the British Green Party's 'weekly payment' would actually be. Obviously to give figures would be pointless, but, according to Irvine and Ponton, 'To be politically attractive, the level of basic income must save people from poverty. Beyond that, it is a matter of careful calculation of what society can afford' (1988, p. 73). The British Green Party simply states that payments would be 'higher than current welfare benefits' (*Manifesto*, 1987, p. 6). Some on the left have criticized this kind of proposal on the grounds that payments would likely be so low as to further institutionalize poverty rather than relieve it. But even if Greens accept that payments might not be as high as some would like, they will maintain that the GBIS's effect of opening up the informal economy and allowing for flexible patterns of work would mean that very few people would remain at GBIS levels of income – and that, if they do, it could be more meaningfully called a voluntary decision than is presently the case.

But it is not of course only a matter of calculation, as Irvine and Ponton suggest, but also of negotiation (and this is the second point to be made), because the Green movement's GBIS proposal is thrown into the political marketplace at a time when social security systems funded by compulsorily raised taxes are under severe intellectual attack. Thus the notion of 'political attractiveness' to which they refer is ambiguous. Those who believe that social security systems encourage idleness will see the GBIS as the height of folly – no one need work at all. Greens are convinced, however, that the vast majority of people will work, and they will argue firmly that at the lower end of the pay-scale the removal of the part-time, unemployment and poverty traps will positively encourage people to work.

The third standard criticism of all guaranteed basic income schemes is that they would be too expensive to put into operation. In response, advocates of such schemes usually take the redistributive bull by the horns and admit that high earners would be expected to finance the GBIS through paying high taxes: one is faced with a graduated income tax system of the type that is currently so out of favour, at least in liberal

[113]

democratic polities. At the same time, Greens can point to all sorts of other taxes that would be levied in the sustainable society: conservation taxes, resource taxes and pollution taxes – all of which they claim would help raise sufficient revenue for the GBIS. Then they will refer to the savings made in administering such a simple system in comparison with the sums spent on present systems; and lastly they will suggest that tax revenues would increase anyway, given the increase in earnings created by more people working.

It seems clear that, in the context of funding, much depends on being able to negotiate higher taxes for higher earners, and in the short term this may be the GBIS's principal drawback. As suggested above, the political culture in most liberal democracies has shifted away from seeing social justice in terms of redistribution, towards something like Robert Nozick's entitlement theory of justice. This theory has it that one is entitled to what one justly owns (e.g. money earned through work) and that it cannot be legitimately taken off you without your consent. From this point of view, taxation is a form of robbery. This, I suggest, is the view that most generally informs attitudes towards taxation today, and funding the GBIS would involve undoing it. This task has proved beyond the capabilities of the left over the last decade and there are no signs, either, that political ecologists have taken this particular problem of persuasion seriously enough.

Two further issues related to the GBIS remain to be raised, both of which bear on the question of how much such schemes have to do with the Green sustainable society anyway. Readers who have taken in the rest of the chapter might feel that the GBIS sits unhappily with the rather radical picture painted up until now of the sustainable society. The GBIS is radical in the sense that it would be a far-reaching extension of present practices, but the point of the Green sustainable society as I have been led to see it is that it constitutes a substantial *break* with present practices. On this reading, we might suggest that there is too much in the GBIS that is 'of this world' to see it as part of a deep-Green solution to sustainability.

Boris Frankel (1987) sounds the first alarm in this regard when he asks what political structures Greens advocate for administering the GBIS. He argues that the centralized nature of such structures stands in tension with the decentralist impulse of the rest of the Green programme. He implies, in other words, that Greens want it both ways – they seek decentralized forms of political life on the one hand and, on the other, they want to institutionalize social practices that are only possible through a high degree of planning and the centralization that that implies. I suspect that Greens will reply that the administration of (and revenue-raising for) the GBIS just will have to be carried out centrally, but that this does not negate the Green principle that 'nothing should be done at a higher level that can be done at a lower' (Porritt, 1986, p. 166). GBIS administration, on this view, does have to be carried out at a 'high level' and that is that. How far one considers this to be a heresy within the Green canon will depend upon how radical one is in one's interpretation of the meaning of 'decentralization' in the Green political pro-gramme. I shall return to this point further below.

More serious in this respect, perhaps, is the objection that the productive system on which the GBIS depends to produce the fabulous amounts of wealth needed to fund it (i.e. the present productive system) is elsewhere described by Greens as being in decline and is unsustainable anyway – that is where Green politics begins, in fact. Put more bluntly, as productivity declines and tax revenues dwindle, where will the money to pay for the GBIS come from? From this perspective, the GBIS looks like a social-democratic measure grafted unsustainably onto the ailing post-industrial body politic, rather than a radically Green measure in the spirit of solutions to the problems of sustain-ability raised by the spectre of limits to growth. At the very least, Greens will find themselves back with the problem of negotiating the redistribution of decreasing amounts of material wealth. Just what social security measures in the Green sustainable society would look like I don't rightly know, but the guaranteed basic income scheme (often the flagship policy of Green political parties) seems to depend too much on the habits and practices of the society that Greens would like to replace to provide the answer.

At the beginning of this chapter I suggested that the limits to growth notion represents the starting-point for Green politics. The notion is indispensable for understanding ecologism, if only because it points us in the direction – at the outset – of the radical prescriptions for political and social life that the Green sustainable society involves. If it were simply a question of eating healthy food, living in a lead-free environment, or using biodegradable detergent, then environmentalist strategies such as green consumerism would probably do the job. But Greens suggest that green consumerism is no more sustainable – in the long run – than grey consumerism: both are subject to limits to growth. This state of affairs needs to be addressed by a specifically different set of habits and practices from those that we presently follow, and green consumerism is too tied in to present rates of depletion, production, consumption and waste to constitute the new set of habits and practices that Greens say we need.

I also suggested that of these four terms – Herman Daly's 'throughput' – consumption was the one on which to focus attention in order best to see from where Green prescriptions take off. The urge to reduce consumption as a response to the limits to growth thesis leads to the development of theories of need, the recommendation to reduce population levels, the questioning of the 'technological fix', the support for sustainable sources of energy – and all this is underpinned by the advocacy of the self-reliant society, the ground-rule for which is provided by Porritt: 'All economic growth in the future must be sustainable: that is to say, it must operate within and not beyond the finite limits of the planet' (1986, p. 120). Having sketched the most important features of the way of life of the sustainable society, from a Green point of view, we are now in a position to consider the (broadly speaking) political–institutional characteristics of such a society. What will it look like?

[116]

Bioregionalism

When I considered the possible responses to the limits to growth thesis nearer the beginning of the chapter, I proposed that we accept Tim O'Riordan's four-fold classification: the 'new global order', the idea of 'centralized authoritarianism', the 'authoritarian commune', and the 'anarchist solution'. Of these four, I suggested that the 'anarchist solution' – 'the self-reliant community modelled on anarchist lines' (O'Riordan, 1981, p. 307) – comes closest to describing what the Green sustainable society would look like. We have seen something of the thoughts that would inform such a society and I can now push the analysis further by considering the notion of bioregionalism. I should stress again that not all Green prescriptions for the sustainable society will take exactly the bioregional form. The best way to read the following few pages is to see that Greens will derive their aspirations from bioregionalism. Put differently, if Greens depart from bioregional principles, the place they eventually arrive at will bear a family resemblance to such principles. Greens will, for example, always advocate decentralized political forms, even if they cannot accept the full centrifugal implications of bioregionalism.

The general principles of what Kirkpatrick Sale has called the 'bioregional paradigm' (1985, pp. 41–132) are simply expressed. We must get to know the land around us, learn its lore and its potential, and live with it and not against it. We must see that living with the land means living in, and according to the ways and rhythms of, its natural regions – its bioregions. There are 'ecoregions' of 'perhaps several hundred thousand square miles' (ibid., p. 56), smaller 'georegions' of a few tens of thousands of square miles, and 'morphoregions' (he has also called these 'vitaregions' – 1984, p. 227) of 'several thousand square miles' (ibid., p. 58). Living bioregionally involves identifying bioregional boundaries and living (for the most part) with what those territories provide in the way of, for example, 'given ores and minerals, woods and leathers, cloths and yarns' (ibid., p. 75). Bioregionalists have identified these regions and have

[117]

names for them: there is a land along the California coast known as Shasta (Tokar, 1987, p. 69).

Within these bioregions people would live in communities because, 'If one were to look for the single basic building block of the ecological world, it would be the community' (Sale, 1985, p. 62). Sale suggests that the 'human animal' has historically favoured communities of 500–1,000 people for face-to-face contact and 5,000–10,000 'for the larger tribal association or extended community' (ibid., p. 64). Communities much bigger than this are regarded as undesirable because they cannot be sustained on their own resources.

The bioregional community would seek to 'minimise resource-use, emphasise conservation and recycling, [and] avoid pollution and waste' (Sale, 1984, p. 230), and all of this would be aimed at achieving sustainability through what Sale calls self-sufficiency. The bioregionalist is likely to be even less keen on trade than the advocate of self-reliance, and Sale himself sees self-sufficiency as centred on a 'full-scale morphoregion' so as to ensure 'a wide range of food, some choice in necessities and some sophistication in luxuries, [and] the population to sustain a university and large hospital and a symphony orchestra' (1985, pp. 74–5). We would, however, be likely to do without some things: 'some bioregions would have to steel themselves for significant changes from their omnivorous and gluttonous habits of the present: noncitrus regions would need to look to other sources of vitamin C, for example' (ibid., p. 75). In general, bioregionalists will claim that the oft-cited problems associated with the unequal endowment of regions with natural resources simply do not, in fact, arise: 'there is not a single bioregion in this country [the United States of America] that would not . . . be able to provide its residents with sufficient food, energy, shelter, and clothing, their own health care and education and arts, their own manufactures and crafts' (ibid.).

Bioregionalists will usually insist that land be communally owned because the fruits of nature are fruits for everyone, and they will urge that polities follow the natural world's example and abhor systems of centralized control: they advocate 'the spreading of power to small and widely dispersed units' (ibid., p. 91). Associated with this is the idea that nature's lesson as far as social relations are concerned is one of equality, or what Sale calls 'complementarity' (ibid., p. 101). The claim – supported by people like Murray Bookchin – is that 'stratification and hierarchy within specific sub-groups in the animal world is extremely rare' (ibid., p. 98), and that, on the basis of what is good for the 'natural' world is good for us as a part of it, hierarchy should not be institutionalized in politics either. One further principle of bioregionalism, that of diversity, will be treated shortly; it has destabilizing possibilities for the picture presented so far.

The guiding principle of bioregionalism then (and, I suggest, for Green politics in general) is that the 'natural' world should determine the political, economic and social life of communities, and that the messages that nature gives off are best read through ecology rather than, say, through social Darwinism: 'by a diligent study of her [nature] . . . we can guide ourselves in constructing human settlements and systems' (Sale, 1984, p. 225). This is in line with what I described as one of the characteristics of ecologism in Chapter 1, and all of the bioregional principles referred to will have their echoes in any form of Green politics. Sustainability is seen as presaged upon reducing the spiritual and material distance between us and the land: 'We must somehow live as close to it [the land] as possible, be in touch with its particular soils, its waters, its winds; we must learn its ways, its capacities, its limits; we must make its rhythms our patterns, its laws our guide, its fruits our bounty' (ibid., pp. 224–5).

This kind of thing provides a good example of a point I made above. No doubt Kirkpatrick Sale's general picture of bioregionalism and the exhortation just quoted both sound extremely far-fetched, but it will certainly inform many of the postures struck by even the least mystical of the Green movement's members. In this particular context nearly all of them will bemoan the lack of knowledge of the land so typical

[119]

of the industrialized human being. They will deplore our ignorance of where our food comes from and how it grows and suggest that the pre-packaged produce on supermarket shelves is both a symptom and a cause of our dangerous distance from the land. In this sense, both they and the bioregionalists will urge us to 'live in place' – to accommodate our lives to the environment in which we live, rather than resisting it.

Agriculture

In this respect, beyond the claims of bioregionalism itself but clearly informed by it, agriculture will always have a special place in the theory and practice of the Green sustainable society – and a particular sort of agriculture at that: 'the problem of how we feed ourselves [is] arguably the most vital component of a Green ecological strategy' (Tokar, 1987, p. 60). This is so in two ways. First there is the relatively well-known point that the Green movement considers present agricultural practices (what they would call 'industrial agriculture') to be unacceptable because unsustainable. Intensive chemical-based farming is held to pollute water-courses, to encourage erosion, to produce tasteless food of low nutritional value, to bring about saliniza-tion of the land through irrigation, to upset ecological balances through insensitive pest control, and to bore us with its monocultural panoramas.

But the Green point pushes past this rather pragmatic attachment to sustainable agriculture. Brian Tokar introduces the idea with the thought that organic farming, in place, would strengthen 'bioregional awareness' (ibid., p. 62). Jonathon Porritt is more explicit. He suggests that the importance of sound agriculture goes beyond producing healthy food on a sustainable basis; rather, 'its implications for a change in the attitude of people to the planet are highly significant. It binds people to the natural processes of the Earth and, with the use of appropriate technology, creates a sense of harmony that is sorely lacking' (1986, p. 180). In this respect, agricultural practices in the Green society are charged with the essential task of providing the site at which our rifts with the 'natural' world are to be healed, and that is why Brian Tokar invests it with such importance. Spirituality ghosts Green politics; Green politics is a filling of the spiritual vacuum at the centre of late-industrial society, and the land itself is the cathedral at which we are urged to worship. Peter Bunyard's message is instructive: 'The search for self-sufficiency is, I believe, as much spiritual and ideological as it is one of trying to reap the basic necessities of life out of the bare minimum of our surroundings' (in Allaby and Bunyard, 1980, p. 26).

In the light of all this we should not be surprised to see that other consequences of sustainable agriculture – such as its labour-intensive nature – have something more than a pragmatic content. Goldsmith reports that 'A rough calculation suggests that it would suffice to increase the agricultural labour force in the UK by four or five times, to enable this country to forgo much of the input of machinery and chemicals which have been introduced over the last thirty years' (1988, p. 197). This urge to produce a population of 'part-time peasants' (Ophuls, 1977, p. 167) is both necessary and desirable, from a Green point of view. It is necessary because sustainable agriculture involves less machinery and therefore more hands, and it is desirable because it is where theory becomes practice – agriculture is, indeed, the praxis of Green politics.

Diversity

One principle of Kirkpatrick Sale's bioregional society has been held over because it is one of the points at which the wider Green movement's notion of the sustainable society will begin to diverge from the bioregional project. The principle is diversity, and the point is that to talk of a generic 'bioregional society' (as I have been doing) is a misrepresentation. More accurately, we have to speak of bioregional *societies* – not only in the obvious numerical sense, but also in terms of their informing political, social and economic characteristics.

Sale writes bluntly that is it not necessarily the case that each bioregional society 'will construct itself upon the values of democracy, equality, liberty, freedom, justice, and other suchlike *desiderata*' (1984, p. 233), and Arne Naess in his 1987 Schumacher lecture agreed with this. This may seem peculiar given Sale's commitment, expressed above, to the notions of equality and political participation, both derived from principles of the science of ecology, but there is evidently a tension between the demands of 'complementarity' and diversity. When diversity is privileged, one is obliged to admit to (and underwrite) the possibility that 'truly autonomous bioregions will likely go their own separate ways and end up with quite disparate political systems – some democracies, no doubt, some direct, some representative, some federative, but undoubtedly all kinds of aristocracies, oligarchies, theocracies, principalities, margravates, duchies and palatinates as well' (ibid.).

At this point the wider Green movement is likely to lose its bioregional nerve. Its members will want to subscribe to Sale's declaration that 'Bioregionalism . . . not merely tolerates but thrives upon the diversities of human behaviour' (ibid., p. 234), but, as images of slavery and sexism come to mind, glassy eyes will snap into focus and Greens will remember that they are as much the heirs of the Enlightenment tradition as its committed critics. They most certainly believe that 'their model of post-industrialism will maximise democracy, freedom, tolerance, equality and other rationalist values which made their appearance in Europe a few hundred years ago' (Frankel, 1987, p. 180), and in this respect the bioregional imperative of diversity is tempered by the desire to universalize messages most often associated with liberal democracy.

Decentralization and its limits

If interpretations of diversity might constitute a point of dispute between bioregionalists and those Greens who would gain inspiration from them, there is one aspect of the bioregional programme that consistently informs Green aspirations – the principle of decentralization. This is always closely linked, too, to the idea of political responsibility being devolved to communities rather than to individuals, either in the strong sense of communities-as-communes, or in the sense of neighbourhood communities at the base of some sort of federative system.

In terms of those most often associated with the Green movement itself, Rudolf Bahro is probably the person most normally linked with full-blown commune recommendations for the shape of the Green society. The reasons he gives for favouring communes echo those given by Sale. In the first place communes are not 'economically expansive'; as Edward Goldsmith puts it: 'to deploy a population in small towns and villages is to reduce to the minimum its impact on the environment' (1972, p. 64). Next, they provide an obvious focus for political decentralization. Third, they are what Bahro calls 'anthropologically favourable', i.e. they correspond more 'to human nature, among other things by avoiding both the neurotic-making family and the alienating big organization' (1986, pp. 87–8). In this respect Goldsmith goes even further: 'it is probable that only in the small community can a man or woman be an individual' (1972, p. 63). Communes therefore provide the site on which personal relationships become fulfilling, and where people will learn to live 'in place' (according to, and not against, their environment).

In this respect, Green politics inserts itself into a tradition that is as long as history and embroils itself in debates that will be most familiar to the modern reader in the context of the theory and practice of communitarian anarchism. Greens (and particularly bioregionalists) bring a novel perspective to bear on this debate in two respects: first, the idea that commune living is somehow 'read off' from the 'natural' world – that it is a natural way of living, and in this sense responds to the demand for sustainability; second, they are also likely to suggest that something like a federation of communes is the

[123]

only viable political–institutional form for the sustainable society to take.

In this sense they will suggest that other political forms are more susceptible to environmental irresponsibility and that this is therefore a very practical reason (in view of the long-term project of sustainability) for supporting the commune option. This is why Goldsmith claims that decentralization is proposed, not 'because we are sunk in nostalgia for a mythical little England of fêtes, olde worlde pubs, and perpetual conversations over garden fences' (ibid., pp. 61–2), but for more hard-headed reasons. The idea is that resource problems are best solved by bringing points of production and consumption closer together – we should no longer be talking of producers and consumers but of 'prosumers'. In other respects, though, the arguments that will surround Green communitarianism are familiar: is it practical? would such a life be stultifying? what would the relationships between communes look like? and so on.

Certainly many will feel uncomfortable at the implications of arbitrary justice implied by Edward Goldsmith's suggestion that 'crime' be controlled 'through the medium of public opinion' by subjecting the offender to 'ridicule' (ibid., p. 135), and will agree with André Gorz that:

> communal autarky always has an impoverishing effect: the more self-sufficient and numerically limited a community is, the smaller the range of activities and choices it can offer to its members. If it has no opening to an area of exogenous activity, knowledge and production, the community becomes a prison . . . only constantly renewed possibilities for discovery, insight, experiment and communication can prevent communal life from becoming impoverished and eventually suffocating. (in Frankel, 1987, p. 59)

The themes of confinement and surveillance at which Gorz hints haunt some Green texts surreptitiously – ('Many in the informal economy who do not now disclose their income . . . would find that in the new system the risks of tax evasion

[124]

outweigh gains' – Irvine and Ponton, 1988, p. 73, for example) – and while this is probably not surprising given the puritanical tenor of much of the Green programme, it is an aspect of Green politics that (on the face of it) can offend the modern liberal sensibility. It seems to me that either Green politics, as a project, will suffer because of this, or it will usefully refer to it as just one more example of the self-denial that sustainable living requires of us. I once knew an anarchist who was surprisingly military about getting people up in the early morning before meetings to wash and clean their teeth. Equally surprisingly, this exercise was generally accepted with good grace because somehow it all seemed part of the necessary preparations for the brave new world that the anarchists were seeking to usher in.

Many Greens, though, will respond to the practical or ethical objections to commune living by falling back on a more loosely conceived notion of political decentralization: the reasons remain the same, but the form is different. I shall suggest, though, that in rejecting the commune approach Greens may come close to allowing the society they want to replace to reappear through the back door in a form that would have been unacceptable to them when they first set out to describe the sustainable society.

The basic rule once the commune option has been set aside, and which we have already seen expressed, is that 'nothing should be done at a higher level that can be done at a lower' (Porritt, 1986, p. 166). This typically turns into a commitment to local politics and some form of participatory democracy: 'Greens believe that many more decisions should be taken at the local level, encouraging greater participation and account-ability', and, in a statement typical of advocates of participatory democracy, 'voting is the *beginning* and not the *end* of one's democratic commitment' (Bunyard and Morgan-Grenville, 1987, pp. 319 and 320). As far as this last is concerned, Brian Tokar refers to New England town meetings as the *locus classicus* of face-to-face democracy in action, as well as to 'ancient Greek democracy, the Parisian sections of the French Revolution, pre-

Revolutionary Boston and the anarchist city of Barcelona during the Spanish Civil War' (1987, pp. 98–9).

This much is clear, and probably familiar. Familiar, too, are the questions normally asked of such a picture, and no one has recently put them more forcefully than Boris Frankel (1987). His principal problem revolves around how such a decentralized society is to be coordinated, in both the political and the economic spheres. We must recognize, of course, that such problems do not arise in the most extreme versions of bioregionalism because contact between communities would not be institutionalized. Or rather, different problems would arise, in the sense that relations between and within communities could not legitimately be universalized and regulated. Frankel wonders in this regard (with reference to Bahro) whether the relationships between decentralized communes would not simply 'grow into capitalist markets with all the inherent qualities of inequality, exploitation and so forth' (ibid., p. 56). But while this could be a problem for Enlightenment enthusiasts, Kirkpatrick Sale and his supporters might consider it merely to be part of life's rich pattern: the outcome of allowing for diversity.

However, if we assume that connections between communes are to be institutionalized, then the relations between local and 'national' levels need to be carefully spelt out. My reading of the Green ideologues' approach to this problem (to the extent that they have dealt with it at all) is that they end up where they do not want to be: with a more weighty 'national' framework than they would like. Taking the economic arena as an example, Greens are typically opposed to the workings of the market as they characterize it. For them, the market unsustainably and therefore irresponsibly encourages consumption, and it most usually is prepared to answer only short-term questions. This, in the context of limits to growth (which by its nature, according to Greens, demands long-term thinking), is unacceptable. The problem in our context is that, if the market is to be fettered, who is to do the fettering? More obviously, if Greens demand long-term policies, we might argue that they will have to be planned and coordinated. Once again, who is to do the planning and coordinating if not some supra-community political agency? As Frankel puts it:

> would a Green post-industrial society minimize or maximize social planning? If it minimized social planning and relied predominantly on market mechanisms, then all the major difficulties of market socialism would appear. If the new society maximized planning, then how would this be possible without national state institutions? (ibid., p. 55)

Once again it is worth stressing that the commune perspective can provide a by-pass of such questions. For Frankel, Bahro takes just this option in that he 'has an idealized image of communal life where there is little need for extensive government-run "social wage" programmes as these jobs and roles will be performed by mutual self-help within the confines of "basic communes" ' (ibid., p. 87). If this option is not taken, though, Greens will respond to Frankel's question in the following way: 'we're talking about establishing at the national level the *minimum legislative framework* necessary for the maintenance of ecological principles, leaving the details to be determined locally' (Bunyard and Morgan-Grenville, 1987, p. 319). The *British Green Party Manifesto* spells out in more detail what this might mean. Here we find that the country would be divided into districts and regions, and that districts would have responsibility for taxation and benefits, social services, housing, education, health care, land reform, policing and aspects of justice, transport and pollution control (1987, p. 16). Central government, on this reading, 'might' retain responsibility for 'foreign affairs, defence, customs and excises, international trade, non-renewable resource conservation and some aspects of justice, transport, pollution control and land reform' (ibid.).

I suggest that the responsibility retained by central government, as suggested here, involves it in much more activity than the original decentralist imperative would have us believe. The

British Green Party Manifesto has a neat solution, for example, to one of the problems that arose in the context of bioregionalism: what about the inequalities of regions – are they to be accepted or somehow modified? The manifesto loses its bioregional nerve in this respect and says that 'a simple and *automatic* formula would be used to redistribute resources between richer and poorer areas' (1987, p. 5). This might be entirely right and proper, but the 'administration of things' is rarely innocent of the exercise of power, and the Green programme, in this respect, seems to invite more than the 'minimum legislative framework' announced by Bunyard and Morgan-Grenville.

This suspicion is certainly borne out in the case of Irvine and Ponton. Loosely, they suggest that central government should be involved in taxing resource-intensive products, providing subsidies for energy conservation, and enforcing performance standards on products (1988, p. 31). More specifically, this seems to result in a plethora of government institutions, miles removed from the light touch, apparently guaranteed by the original decentralist project:

> A department of resource conservation and planning would be a necessary agency to look after the measures that require government action. It would, for example, plan how much of a particular mineral was needed in a given year while a ministry of land use would determine the best sites for extraction. The ministries of environment protection and of health would ensure that this was done in ways which had the least impact on place and people. (ibid.)

This sounds much more like a parody of a heavy-industrial command economy than a recipe for post-industrial decentralized sustainability. The conclusion we reach is that, if the radical commune solution in which relations are voluntary, unsupervised and non-universalizable is rejected, then the Green regulatory framework is in danger of appearing as rigid and as interventionist as that which it seeks to supersede. We might even go so far as to say that, at this point, what I (through O'Riordan) characterized near the beginning of the chapter as the best description of the Green sustainable society – 'the self-reliant community based on anarchist lines' – has been betrayed in favour of O'Riordan's second category: centralized authoritarianism. If this is the case, then we are no longer talking about Green politics.

CHAPTER 4

Strategies for Green change

How do we start? By what imaginable transition can we move from here to a green future? Can the immense gap at least be narrowed, between the Green-thinking dreamers and the present reality? (Schwarz and Schwarz, 1987, p. 253)

Ecologism provides us with a critique of current patterns of production and consumption, and the Schwarzs' 'Green-thinking dreamers' referred to in the quotation above have painted pictures of the sustainable society that they would like us to inhabit. Two of the classic requirements of a functional definition of 'ideology' are thus far fulfilled by ecologism: it has a description (which is already an interpretation) of 'political reality', and it has a prescription for the future, which amounts to a description of the Good Life. In the light of the space between the former and the latter, the primary question addressed in this chapter is: what is ecologism's strategy for social change? The subsidiary question posed is: will this strategy (or these strategies) do the job required of them?

The first point to note about ecologism and social change is that very little serious thinking has been done about it. Boris Frankel has rightly observed that: 'one reads very little about how to get there from here' (1987, p. 227), and it is noticeable how many conversations about Green politics very soon dry up when the issue of change is broached. Several reasons for the lack of material might be advanced.

In the first place there is the belief that the changes required are so far-reaching that nothing short of an environmental catastrophe could produce the political will needed to bring them about: 'it is quite "unrealistic" to believe that we shall choose simplicity and frugality except under ecological duress' (Daly, 1977a, p. 170).

Second, amongst more optimistic observers there has been a tendency (noted in Chapter 1) to believe that the delivery of the message of impending catastrophe would be enough to generate social change. After all, how could a humanity aware of the threat to its existence fail to act in its own best interests? This certainly seems to have been the line taken in the original *Limits to Growth* report: 'We believe that an unexpectedly large number of men and women of all ages and conditions will readily respond to the challenge and will be eager to discuss not *if* but *how* we can create this new future' (Meadows *et al.*, 1974, p. 196). Contrary to its authors' expectations, however, the publication of their report has not of itself produced the changes for which they argue.

It is often the immaturity of the ideology that is held responsible for its not having got to grips with the issue of social change: Green thinkers have had their work cut out simply describing our environmental malaise and convincing us of their arguments. It follows, from this perspective, that the very newness of the ideology is the reason for its current lack of a strategy that might be productive in the light of the ends it proposes. Now that the foundations are more or less in place, it is held, the strategy will follow.

This argument would be more persuasive if ecologism really *did* have no strategy for social change. The point is, rather, that it does have various strategies, but we harbour the suspicion that they are all being found wanting – it is not as though its strategies are correct and that they just need more time to work. Jonathon Porritt sets the agenda for this chapter: 'Though the environmental movement has indeed been growing in strength over the past few years, so that its influence is now greater than it has been since the early 1970s, this has not brought about the kind of fundamental shift that one might have anticipated' (in Goldsmith and Hildyard, 1986, p. 343). Porritt goes on to argue that this is because the Green movement has founded its project on reform of the system rather than its 'radical overhaul'. This might be true, but it simply pushes the problem back one space and the problem still remains: how is the radical overhaul to be brought about? It must be stressed, though, that 'radical overhaul' is what we are talking about. No one would dispute that significant improvements to the environment can be brought about by parliamentary party and pressure group activity – it would be a mistake to underestimate the achievements of groups like Friends of the Earth, brought about by high levels of commitment and undeniable expertise. However, Porritt's concern at the lack of change is based on his desire for a 'fundamental shift' and it is this objective, rather than merely environmental ones, that provides the backdrop for this chapter.

The distinction around which I intend to organize the discussion is that between parliamentary and extra-parliamentary political activity. There is evidently nothing particularly novel about this, although the very fact that this turns out to be the most fruitful way of approaching the issue is symptomatic of the general theme of ecologism and social change: that liberal–democratic politics and the spaces in which it allows one to act constitute the parameters for the majority of ecological political action.

Action through and around the legislature

Green movements in most countries are attached to recognizably Green parties, which attempt to seek election to national legislatures. Green movements in all countries that have one see it as at least part of their role to try to influence the legislative process, either while policy is being drawn up, while bills are being debated, or during their execution. The principal assumption behind both kinds of activity (broadly speaking, party political activity and pressure group activity) is that the liberal–democratic decision-making process and the economic structures with which it is engaged are sufficiently open to allow the Green agenda to be fulfilled through them. It seems to be accepted that even if a Green party is not elected to government then sufficient pressure can be brought to bear on the incumbents to bring about a sustainable society:

> The Government . . . must intervene, using the full range of sticks and carrots at its disposal, to address the root causes of our current crisis, not the symptoms. Through legislation, direct regulation, changes in the taxation system, subsidies, grants, loans, efficiency standards, the Government has it in its power to effect the sort of transition I am talking about. (Porritt, 1986, p. 133)

The great majority of Green literature on the issue of strategies for political change is written in the same vein. Peter Bunyard and Fern Morgan-Grenville's *The Green Alternative*, which is very widely read in and around the Green movement, is typical. The following constitutes a representative sample of the advice given (my emphasis added in each case): 'If we act immediately, through *lobbying local councils* and rallying support amongst the community, we may be able to save areas of beauty for ourselves and the rest of humanity' (1987, p. 1); 'We should *lobby parliament* and voice concern that our money, via taxes, is being used to perpetrate policies that are ultimately destructive' (p. 30); 'We must make our own voices heard through, for instance, *informing our MPs*' (p. 34); '*write to your MP*' (pp. 58, 89). It is important to understand that these are not isolated examples of the kind of strategy advanced by the Green movement. On the contrary, at this level the movement's prescriptions rely extremely heavily on operation within the liberal–democratic framework. The question is: is such reliance advisable given the radical political and social change that the Green movement proposes?

The first problem for any Green party (in some countries, and certainly in Britain) is that of getting elected in the first place

– by which I mean not necessarily being elected to government but garnering sufficient votes to gain even minimal representation in the legislature. In Britain the first-past-the-post system, in which the candidate in a given constituency with the most number of votes takes the seat, militates notoriously against small parties. The results of such a system were most obviously on view in the 1989 European elections when the British Green Party gained 15 per cent of the popular vote and yet won no seats in the Strasbourg parliament. It is extremely hard to imagine the British Parliament with even one Green representative, let alone with sufficient members to be able to enter into coalition with one of the major parties (a doubtful strategy in any case). Of course most members of the Green Party in Britain are aware of this, and the parliamentary candidates I have talked to are evidently serious about political power, but see their role principally in educative terms. The platform provided by elections is used to 'get the message across'. Of course, not all countries make it so difficult for small parties to taste electoral success, and shortly I shall consider the situation where a Green party does have representation in a national legislature.

In any case, a Green party's political problems clearly do not end with getting elected. It would be faced with confronting and overcoming the constraints imposed by powerful interests intent on preventing the radical political and social change that a Green government would seek. Even at the level of relatively minor changes, opposition would most likely be intense. Werner Hülsberg, for example, discusses the notion of a Green government taxing resource-intensive industries and observes that 'the question of power is largely ignored in this approach' (1988, p. 182), and that 'it [is] clear that attempts at structural reform would be met with an investment strike and flight of capital' (ibid., p. 183). The central question in this context is whether a sustainable society can be brought about through the use of existing state institutions.

It has been argued that from two points of view the answer would seem to be No. In the first place, political institutions are not best seen as neutral instruments that can be used by just any operator to achieve just any political ends. Political institutions are always already tainted by precisely those strategies and practices that the Green movement, in its radical pretensions, seeks to replace. An instance of this would be the way in which political institutions (in the Western world at least) have come to embody the principles of representative forms of democracy. These institutions represent the formal abandonment of notions of mass participation in political life; they are indeed 'designed' to *preclude* the possibility of massive regular participation.

The exclusive nature of these institutions, which is constitutive of them, makes it impossible for them to be used for inclusive ends. If they were to be inclusive, in the sense of participatory, then they would be something other than they are. On this reading, participatory politics demands the radical restructuring (if not the abolition) of present institutions rather than their use in the service of participation. Attempts to press them into such service will necessarily result in the progressive dilution of the original project. Jonathon Porritt has argued that 'the taking of power from below, by this process of self-empowerment, must be combined with the passing down of power from above' (1986, p. 167), or as the Ecology Party's 1983 manifesto put it: 'The power of parliament should be diminished by a process of gradual devolution' (*British Ecology Party Manifesto*, 1983, Section AD [Public Administration and Government] 310). It has been suggested that this is a Utopian strategy, not because Greens are as likely to be corrupted by power as anyone else (although this is a respectable argument), but because the institutions Porritt proposes to use already have centralization built into them.

Secondly, we have to take into account Hülsberg's point that political change is a matter of political and economic power. Even if we assume a Green party in government, we are still left with the problem of powerful sources of resistance in other institutions such as the bureaucracy, the financial centres and so on. The *die Grünen* Sindelfingen programme of January 1983

[135]

expressed the hopeful belief that 'the desire for a different kind of life and work will grip the majority, and that this majority will be strong enough to demonstrate clearly to the opposing minority the superiority of an economic system whose goal is not itself but ecological and social need' (Hülsberg, 1988, p. 127). Hülsberg himself cogently observes that, in this formulation, 'The question as to what would happen if the "opposing minority" could not be convinced is simply avoided' (ibid.).

Moreover, avoidance of this question seems to be standard procedure in and around the Green movement. Jonathon Porritt envisages a moment when a series of interests bent on maintaining the status quo comes into conflict with 'human power' (i.e. the Green movement) and comments, 'Whether this power block is going to be sufficiently strong to overcome the first power block – I wouldn't like to conjecture' (in Schwarz and Schwarz, 1987, pp. 259–60). It is hard to see the point of not conjecturing, precisely because the success of the Green project will probably depend on a strategy to overcome the opposition that Porritt predicts.

I suspect that Porritt's reluctance is explained at least in part by the fact that the thought of what to do with intransigent opposition leads to considerations of the possibility of violence accompanying political change. It is a strongly held Green maxim that means for change should be consistent with the ends intended. This argument is invariably deployed against prescriptions for violent political change, and is probably one of the reasons for Porritt's 'refusal to conjecture'. It might be pointed out that this position makes selective use of the means–ends argument. Why should the contemplation of the use of violence be any less consistent with the means–ends maxim than the use of institutions and strategies that were born out of, and have subsequently buttressed, unsustainable social practices? It was mentioned above that the use of such institutions would be likely to lead to the colonization, and thus betrayal, of the original Green project. In this sense, the means that the Green movement proposes to employ are no more consistent with its ends than the putative use of violence. One might argue that the very selectivity of the Green use of the means–ends maxim shows that it has already succumbed to colonization at the very moment of attempting decolonization.

I promised earlier to discuss the situation of a Green party that had significant representation in a national legislature, so as to illustrate the problems encountered there. *Die Grünen* in West Germany provide us with a set of experiences to which we can usefully refer: in the federal elections of 1983 they obtained 5.6 per cent of the vote and entered the Bundestag, increasing their share of the vote to 8.3 per cent in the next election of January 1987. The metaphor of colonization introduced above allows us to theorize some of the experiences of *die Grünen* since 1983, for in two specific contexts the party has been colonized by the demands and temptations of parliamentary activity.

In the first place, enormous amounts of energy have been expended over the issue of whether to make tactical alliances with other political parties so as to influence policy in a more extensive way. The history of this debate is well documented in the books of Fritjof Capra and Charlene Spretnak (1986) and Werner Hülsberg (1988), and in E. Gene Frankland's (1988) article, and need not be repeated here. The crucial observation is that of Petra Kelly: 'If the Greens end up becoming merely ecological Social Democrats, then the experiment is finished – it will have become a waste' (in Capra and Spretnak, 1986, p. 152). Any Green party operating in the parliamentary sphere will be faced, at some level of administration, with the possibility of coalition. Kelly's warning is clear: that dealings with other parties are undertaken at the risk of dilution of properly Green principles. In this sense, the demands of parliamentary politics can contribute to a wearing down of the Green project and the consequent likelihood of the abandonment of the project as originally conceived.

This has been borne out concretely in the second instance to which I want to refer: the struggle over the rotation system of delegates elected to the Bundestag. Under this system, Green representatives elected to the Bundestag would serve only two

[137]

years and then give way for the next two years to understudies who were originally hired as 'legislative assistants' (Capra and Spretnak, 1986, p. 39). The reason given for this principle reflects the fear of colonization: 'Because a person's thinking is affected by the way she or he lives, eight, or even four years in the Bundestag – or a state legislature – machine would be very destructive' (ibid.). At the same time, the rotation system was intended to be a visible sign of Green refusal to concentrate political power in the hands of relatively few individuals. Objections to the principle were derived from the demands of working effectively in the Bundestag: rotation was held to prevent the emergence of influential 'personalities', and it reduced expertise.

Since 1983 commitment to rotation and the principles it embodies waned and in May 1986 it was formally abandoned. This is not because the principles in themselves were found wanting but because they were unworkable, as originally conceived, in the context of parliamentary politics: 'Under the pressure of political developments, naive notions of rank and file democracy are now a thing of the past' (Hülsberg, 1988, p. 123). In similar vein Capra and Spretnak state that 'the rotation principle for elected officials has proven to be more trouble than it is worth for the Greens in West Germany' (1986, pp. 188–9). The judgements of 'worth' and 'naivete' are made entirely from within the context of parliamentary politics, and my question is: how far can Green politics be achieved through that context if it demands the progressive abandonment of the principles of such politics?

In 1985 Rudolf Bahro, the most famous 'fundamentalist' in *die Grünen*, left the party. He argued that by then the party had 'no basic ecological position' because 'what people are trying to do . . . is to save a party – no matter what kind of party, and no matter for what purpose. The main thing is for it to get re-elected to parliament in 1987' (1986, p. 210). Bahro is here articulating the experience of a fundamentalist Green who has seen the party colonized by the demands of the very system that it originally sought to overcome. His conclusion ran as follows:

At last I have understood that a party is a counterproductive tool, that the given political space is a trap into which life energy disappears, indeed, where it is rededicated to the spiral of death. This is not a general but a quite concrete type of despair. It is directed not at the original project which is today called 'fundamental', but at the party. I've finished with it now. (ibid., p. 211)

The problem that has informed this discussion of the possibility of bringing about Green change through the parliamentary process centres on the difficulty of bringing about a decolonized society through structures that are already colonized – structures that are deeply (perhaps irremediably) implicated in the status quo that Green politics seeks to shift. This is not a new problem: socialists have been debating the issue for over 150 years. I think it important to reiterate it in this context, though, because it points up the tension between the radical nature of the Green project and the piecemeal strategy that has been developed to bring it about. Indeed if one focused solely on the parliamentary strategy one could be forgiven for thinking that the Green movement had no radical project beyond environmentalism at all, so far is this strategy removed from any radical pretensions. Raymond Williams has pointed out the dangers of the 'practical surrender of the real agenda of issues to just that version of politics which the critique has shown to be defective and is offering to supersede' (1986, pp. 252–3). This is the point of the general critique of the parliamentary road to the sustainable society.

Most people in the Green movement who argue for change through liberal–democratic political structures will also support other forms of action. The rest of this chapter will be taken up with discussing these other options, under the three headings of lifestyle, communities and class.

Lifestyle

The general principle behind both lifestyle and community strategies is that of arguing for a change of consciousness leading to changes in behaviour at both the individual and community level. It is proposed that political change will only occur once people think differently or, more particularly, that sustainable living must be prefaced by sustainable thinking. As the label suggests, lifestyle change thus concerns changes in the patterns of individual behaviour in daily life. Typical examples of this would be: care with the things you buy, the things you say, where you invest your money, the way you treat people, the transport you use and so on.

There has been a veritable explosion in the popularity of green lifestyle changes in Britain in recent months. Home ecology, among certain sections of the community at least, is all the rage. Retailers have picked up and reinforced this trend and the major supermarket chains, in particular, are falling over themselves to stock their shelves with environmentally friendly goods. Products in green packets sell significantly better than similar products packaged in any other colour. In this context, green has rapidly become the colour of capitalist energy and enterprise. From the point of view of lifestyle changes, the spaces for political action are in principle infinite – even the toilet is a potential locus for radical politics, for as John Seymour and Herbert Girardet inform us: 'A quarter of all domestic water in most countries goes straight down the toilet. Every time somebody flushes the toilet about 20 litres of water are instantly changed from being pure to being polluted' (1987, p. 27). They offer concise advice: 'If it's brown wash it down. If it's yellow let it mellow' (ibid.). I suppose that's one way to start a revolution.

This kind of strategy has been around for a long time in the Green movement and it has spawned an enormous number of books and pamphlets on practical action to avert environmental decay. Back in 1973 Fritz Schumacher wrote, 'Everywhere people ask: "What can I actually *do*?" The answer is as simple as it is disconcerting: we can, each of us, work to put our own inner house in order' (1976, pp. 249–50). The theme is consistent: that personal transformation of consciousness leads to altered individual behaviour, which in turn can be translated into sustainable community living: 'The only possible building blocks of a Greener future are individuals moving towards a Greener way of life *themselves* and joining together with others who are doing the same' (Bunyard and Morgan-Grenville, 1987, p. 336).

The positive aspect of this strategy is that some individuals do indeed end up living sounder, more ecological lives. More bottles and newspapers are recycled, more lead-free petrol is bought, and less harmful detergents are washed down the plughole. The disadvantage, though, is that the world around goes on much as before, unGreened and unsustainable – certainly in terms of Porritt's desire for a 'radical overhaul', which I took as my rubric for this chapter. In the first place one has the problem of persuading sufficient numbers of people to lead sustainable lives for it to make a difference to the integrity of the environment. It is evidently hard to predict just how far the message will spread, and how many people will act on it, but it seems unlikely that a massive number of individuals will experience the conversion that will lead to the necessary changes in their daily behaviour.

At the same time, many of the proposals for change of this sort ask us to alter our behaviour at particular points in our daily life and then allow us back on the unsustainable rampage. There is nothing inherently Green, for example, in green consumerism, briefly referred to above. It is true that consumer pressure helped bring about a reduction in the use of CFCs in aerosol sprays. It is true that the Body Shop will supply you with exotic perfumes and shampoos in reusable bottles and that have not been tested on animals. It is true that we can help extend the life of tropical rainforests by resisting the temptation to buy mahogany toilet seats. None of these activities should be belittled as actions to help save the environment, and they are particularly important in that they show it is possible to do something. However, the consumer strategy is arguably counter-productive at a deeper level of Green analysis.

First, it does nothing to confront the central Green point that unlimited production and consumption – no matter how environmentally friendly – is impossible to sustain in a limited system. The problem here is not so much to get people to consume soundly but to get them – or at least those living in profligate societies – to consume less. The Body Shop strategy is a hymn to consumption: in their contribution to the Friends of the Earth Green Consumer Week leaflet (12–18 September 1988) they urge people to 'wield their purchasing power responsibly' rather than to wield it less often. It is this that makes green consumerism environmental rather than Green.

Second, it has been pointed out that 'there are masses of people who are disenfranchised from this exercise of power by virtue of not having the money to spend in the first place' (*Green Line*, no. 60, March 1988, p. 12). Third, the Green movement has always felt consumerism to be too grubby and materialistic a means to lead us reliably to the stated end of a society of 'voluntary simplicity'. This is the point behind Porritt and Winner's observation that 'A crude, consumer-driven culture prevails, in which the spirit is denied and the arts are rejected or reduced to a privileged enclave for the few' (1988, p. 247) and, more generally, that 'it is . . . worth stressing that the underlying aim of this green consumerism is to *reform* rather than fundamentally restructure our patterns of consumption' (ibid., p. 199). Once more we are forced to recognize the difference between environmentalism and ecologism: the strategy of green consumerism, in its call for change substantially in line with present strategies based on unlimited production and consumption, is a child of the former rather than the latter.

The strategy of change in individual habits leading to long-term social change takes no account, either, of the problem of political power and resistance to which I referred in the previous section. It is perhaps unrealistic to assume that those forces that would be positively hostile to sustainability will allow present forms of production and consumption to wither away. Of course this is much less of a problem if the Green movement has in mind only some form of attenuated environmentalism, but if (once again) it is serious about the desire to usher in the

[142]

kind of society described in Chapter 3 then it will eventually be forced to confront the issue of massive resistance to change.

What seems common to these lifestyle strategies as I have treated them is that they mostly reject the idea that bringing about change is a properly 'political' affair – they do not hold that Green change is principally a matter of occupying positions of political power and shifting the levers in the right direction. Lifestyle strategies take seriously the idea that profound changes in attitudes are a precondition for social and political change. In Chapter 1 it was noted that spirituality is of much greater importance to the Green perspective than is probably publicly realized, and this has made a significant impression on some activists in the movement with regard to how change might come about. Rudolf Bahro's writings from the period of his increasing disillusionment with *die Grünen* and the parliamentary strategy are the *locus classicus* of what we might tentatively call the 'religious approach' to Green change.

The general point behind the religious approach is that the changes that need to take place are too profound to be dealt with in the political arena, and that the proper territory for action is the psyche rather than the parliamentary chamber. This approach takes seriously the point made above – namely, that political opposition to Green change would be massive – and sidesteps it. Bahro talks expressively of needing to take 'a new run-up from so far back that we can't afford to waste our time in the mock battles which are so typical of Green committees' (1986, p. 159), and the change he envisages is the 'metaphysical reconstruction' advocated by Jonathon Porritt and David Winner (1988, pp. 246–9).

Ultimately this approach involves a rejection of political strategies, normally understood, on the basis of the belief that profound shifts of direction are carried out only by those motivated by what we might loosely call a religious, rather than a material, sense: 'The differentiation between the creative forces and the forces of inertia does not take place economically or sociologically but rather psychologically and in the last instance religiously' (Bahro, 1986, p. 94). Such a belief, in Bahro's case, is based upon a particular reading of history:

> If we take a look in history at the foundations on which new cultures were based or existing ones essentially changed, we always come up against the fact that in such times people returned to those strata of consciousness which are traditionally described as religious. (ibid., p. 90)

This is, of course, in direct opposition to any theory that has it that political and social change is primarily generated through people identifying their immediate material (widely understood) interests and acting to satisfy them. Bahro's contention causes him to take completely seriously the idea that Porritt's metaphysical reconstruction will involve revisiting the historical experience to which he refers: 'We need a new Benedictine order', he writes (ibid., p. 90). Part of his enthusiasm for the Benedictine experience lies in its having taken a communal form, and we have already seen him (in Chapter 3) arguing that the sustainable society will be founded upon small-communal life. But in our present context the content of Benedictine life is more important than the context within which it was lived. Very significantly, Bahro writes that 'the monastery was not meant as an economic microcosm to be indefinitely multiplied. Its "service" as forerunner related to the *inward arrangement* of the feudal world' (ibid., p. 94; emphasis added).

In other words, the function of the monastery was not so much to advertize a different form of life as to create pockets of existence in which its content, or its psychological dispositions, had changed. Bahro's contention is that a modern-day Benedictine-style movement would provide the points of light and the conversionary zeal necessary to engineer the changes required by what he conceives to be the profundity of the present crisis. The missionary sense is never far away: 'there should be some initiators (men and women) who make a personal decision, begin by preparing themselves and a project and gather around them a circle of fellow-strivers' (ibid., p. 91). The end result, hopes Bahro, would be an overbalancing of the spirit in favour of Green reconstruction:

> The accumulation of spiritual forces . . . will at a particular point in time which can't be foreseen exceed a threshold size. Such a 'critical mass', once accumulated, then acquires under certain circumstances a transformative influence over the whole society. (ibid., p. 98)

Bahro has been roundly criticized for sentiments such as this, not least because it has led him into the dubious gold-plated Rolls-Royce world of Bhagwan Shree Rajneesh in California. But the merit of his position is that it takes the spiritual dimension of Green politics absolutely seriously. I argued in Chapter 2 that there was a gulf between spirituality (in the guise of deep ecology) and politics in the theory and practice of the Green movement, and suggested that the spirituality ought to come to meet the politics. Bahro would reject this approach, saying that if the politics is out of step with the spirit, then the spirit must take precedence over the politics. In this sense Green change might properly involve vacating the corridors of power and occupying the hotly disputed space around spiritual sites such as Stonehenge, or exchanging the pin-striped suit for the druid's gown. And if the extent of the threat to an established way of life is in direct proportion to the violence of the reaction to it of the forces of law and order, then, judging by the last several summer solstice celebrations at Stonehenge, Bahro and his supporters may well have a point.

Communities

A general problem with the strategy of lifestyle change is that it is ultimately divorced from where it wants to go, in that it is not obvious how the individualism on which it is based will convert into the communitarianism that is central to most

[145]

descriptions of the sustainable society. (This problem is less acute in Bahro's case, described above, because the change in consciousness that he prescribes is already tied to community living.) It would appear more sensible to subscribe to forms of political action that are already communitarian, and that are therefore both a practice and anticipation of the advertised goal. In this sense the future is built into the present and the programme is therefore more intellectually convincing and practically coherent.

In this context Robyn Eckersley has argued that 'The revolutionary subject is . . . the active, responsible person-in-community, *homo communitas*, if you like' (1987, p. 19). She goes on to suggest, in a vein referred to above, that this is because 'Perhaps the ultimate principle of ecopraxis is the need to maintain consistency between means and ends' (ibid., p. 21). Consequently, 'The most revolutionary structures are seen to be those that foster the development of self-help, community responsibility and free activity and are consistent with the ecotopian ideal of a loose federation of regions and communes' (ibid., p. 22).

Community strategies might be an improvement on lifestyle strategies, then, because they are already a practice of the future in a more complete sense than that allowed by changes in individual behaviour patterns. They are more clearly an alternative to existing norms and practices, and, to the extent that they work, they show that it is possible to live differently – even sustainably. Rudolf Bahro has expressed it as follows: 'To bring it down to the basic concept, we must build up areas liberated from the industrial system. That means, liberated from nuclear weapons and from supermarkets. What we are talking about is a new social formation and a different civilisation' (1986, p. 29).

Obviously not just any communities will do. It is not enough to say that 'a major priority for both reds and greens is the campaign to win for communities, greater control over their environment' (Weston, 1986, p. 160), without those communities having a clear idea of how they might operate sustainably. In this context the kinds of communities that advertise for ecological lifestyles are rural self-sufficiency farms, city farms, some workers' co-operatives, some kinds of squat throughout the cities of Europe, and, more concretely (in Britain), the Centre for Alternative Technology (CAT) at Machynlleth in Wales and the Findhorn community in Scotland.

The Schwarzes have observed that 'these ventures operate outside and potentially in opposition to, the prevailing culture' (1987, p. 73), and with that they may have put their finger on the necessary defining characteristic of any strategy that hopes to bring about radical change. In the section on parliamentary change, it was suggested that initiatives in and around the legislature were too easily absorbed, and thus neutralized, by their context. Initiatives that live 'outside' the prevailing culture and its diversionary channels have a much brighter chance of remaining oppositional and therefore of bringing about radical change.

However, even this needs to be qualified because 'to be outside' and 'to be oppositional' are not the same thing, and the difference is crucial in terms of understanding the options for Green political strategy. This is because it can be argued that the dominant set of modes and practices needs an opposition against which to define itself and with respect to which to judge itself. In this sense the polarity that opposition sets up helps to sustain and reproduce that which it opposes. One can see this phenomenon in operation at the Centre for Alternative Technology in Wales. At the outset the community at the Centre intended to be 'outside' the prevailing culture, independent of the National Electricity Grid and living a daily life organized around radically democratic and sustainable principles: 'low-tech methods, reduced or simplified methods of consumption, job-rotation, personal growth, priority to collective resources, blurring the distinction of work/non-work, a strong emphasis on community life, and "living the technology" ' (Harper, n.d., p. 4). But, as the same member of the community put it, 'Gradually the bloom faded. I watched it happen in myself. A combination of hard experience, exhaustion, human frailty, pressures of family life, a desire to be acceptable to ordinary humanity, ageing . . . turned me into a reluctant moderate' (ibid., p. 2).

This must be the story of a thousand alternative communities that have found that opposition ends up at incorporation. Now the CAT processes thousands of visitors a year who come from all over the world and pay money to look in on an experiment that, by virtue of the visitors themselves, is shown to have lapsed. Peter Harper writes, 'Sadly, but inevitably, I see a time of Revisionism ahead . . . The Quarry [the Centre is built in an old slate quarry] will become more efficient, harmonious, consistent, respectable, and boring. It will be a successful institution, not a community' (ibid., p. 6). The Centre now is a successful institution – that which was decolonized has been recolonized, and we are left to celebrate 'the Quarry's arrival as a respectable and integral part of British society' (ibid., p. 7).

Of course it might be argued that it is precisely this respectability that is now the Centre's strongest card in the context of persuading visitors to go home and practise the kind of lifestyle change described above. Some might even be so taken by the lifestyle of the community's members that they go and set up their own communities – and if this were to happen to sufficient people (although there is no evidence that it has) it would amount to justification of the strategy of change by example. The CAT's respectability, it is suggested, makes it a likely source of inspiration in that it is recognizably similar to 'our' society: they have telephones and a restaurant, they care about being warm, and they are surrounded by technology, some of it makeshift but some of it extremely complex. The members' daily lives do not appear to revolve around long periods of meditation, shamanistic rituals or talking to lettuces, and so the day visitor is less likely to dismiss the community as irrelevant to her or his own experience. I am sure this is true, but one is still confronted with the distinction between environmental and fully Green change. The CAT's success will lie in raising an environmental consciousness rather than in providing a 'liberated zone' (in Rudolf Bahro's evocative phrase) of sustainable living, and this is the distinction Harper was pointing to in describing the Centre as a 'successful institution' rather than a 'community'.

Most community initiatives, then, oppose the prevailing culture rather than live outside it. Just what 'living outside' means, and how far it is even possible, will be discussed shortly, but it seems clear that part of the reason why community initiatives have not brought about the 'fundamental shift' that Jonathon Porritt mentioned at the beginning of the chapter is because their opposition is easily neutralized and, indeed, turns out to be necessary for the very survival and reproduction of that which it opposes.

What I have called community strategies are arguably an improvement on lifestyle change because they make more ready connections between present practice and future aspirations. However, besides easy neutralization, such strategies depend too heavily (like their lifestyle counterparts) on change by example. They may indeed show us that sustainable styles of life are possible, but as agents for political change they rely entirely on their seductive capacity. The problem is that people refuse to be seduced: rather than producing radical changes in consciousness, sustainable communities perform the role of the surrogate good conscience, and we can go at the weekend to see it operating.

If confrontation appears to result so easily in co-option, then perhaps circumvention is another way forward for the Green movement. I have suggested that the principal advantage of community strategies for change is that they anticipate the advertised Green future, particularly its decentralized communitarian aspects. In this context an interesting practice has recently reappeared, which depends not upon setting up entirely integral communities, but upon allowing communities of work and exchange to 'emerge' through creating a system of what is most generally referred to as 'local money'.

Such systems are by no means new and they have usually appeared when local economies stagnate owing to the flight of capital or the under-utilization of local skills and resources. The results of such a situation are familiar:

> When local unemployment rises, for whatever reason, people lose their incomes and have less money in their pockets. They spend less money with local traders, who in turn have less money in their pockets, then the whole local economy takes a downturn and becomes sluggish. Unemployed people sit at home while shopkeepers watch half-empty shops. The economic activity which should be the lifespring of an economy begins to dry up. (Dauncey, 1988, p. 51)

The aim of a local money system is therefore both to return a measure of control of currency to the community and to put dormant skills and resources back into circulation. The results sometimes seem to have been spectacular:

> In the town of Worgl, Austria, there stands a bridge whose plaque commemorates the fact that it was built by debt-free, locally created money. This was just a small part of a significant experiment that transformed towns and whole areas out of poverty within three months and into prosperity within one year, at a time when there was widespread unemployment in the national economy. (Weston in Ekins, 1986, p. 199)

This particular experiment took place between about 1929 and 1934 and, significantly, was ended when 200 Austrian mayors met and decided to follow Worgl's example, whereupon the Austrian National Bank began a long legal battle to have the scheme outlawed. They eventually succeeded and the system was wound up.

Probably the best-known contemporary example of a local money scheme is the Local Employment and Trade System (LETSystem), which has been running in the town of Courtenay on Canada's Vancouver Island since 1983. The general principles are as follows:

> A number of people who live locally and who want to trade together get together, agree to the LETSystem rules, and give

themselves account numbers. Each person then makes out two lists, one of 'wants' and another of 'offers', with prices attached (following normal market prices). A joint list is made up and circulated to everyone. Then the members look down the list, phone whoever has what they want, and start trading . . . The limits of one-to-one barter are eliminated, as you can now trade with the people in the system as a whole: barter is now a collective proposition. (Dauncey, 1988, p. 52)

No money changes hands because there is no actual 'money' – credits and debits are recorded on a computer and the Green dollars in which LETSystem users trade never get beyond being intangible bits of information. If I sell a car for, say, 2000 Green dollars, then the computer credits me with those dollars, which I can then use within – and only within – the system. The money thus remains within the system-community and provides the incentive for people to advertise, sell and buy skills and resources. Shopkeepers may decide to sell their goods wholly or partly in Green dollars, and so benefit from the newly generated buying-power of LETSystem users.

This is not the place to go into the details of local money experiments and the problems that can come with them: hoarding, inflation, tax liability, social security implications, defaulting on debits by leaving the 'community', and so on. Likewise I have mentioned only two of the more obvious advantages of such a system in a run-down local economy: money stays local and incentive is provided to exercise skills that might otherwise remain dormant. LETSystem users have reported other benefits, such as simplicity, the personal nature of transactions, and the building of self-confidence that comes with supplying others with goods and services they require.

My intention here has simply been to show how local money schemes might be considered as one potential strategy for Green change – a 'community' strategy in my typology in that they anticipate the decentralized communitarian nature of the sustainable society. At the same time though, the Austrian National Bank's reaction to the Worgl experiment described above might be taken as a sign of the potentially subversive nature of local money schemes. They appear to be less easily co-opted than other examples of community change, and in this respect have characteristics that might well qualify them as a part-strategy for the possible agents of change discussed in the following section.

Class

The basic problem with both lifestyle and community change is that the question of *how* the necessary change of consciousness is to be brought about is not confronted, or at least, when it is, it is not adequately resolved.

The simple 'change of consciousness' position often has the character of a religious conversion, and in the following quotation from Arnold Toynbee, cited approvingly by Jonathon Porritt, this is made explicit: 'The present threat to mankind's survival can be removed only by a revolutionary change of heart in individual human beings. This change of heart must be inspired by religion in order to generate the will power needed for putting arduous new ideals into practice' (1986, p. 211). Generally speaking this kind of sentiment is accompanied by an exhortation to education as a necessary preface to conversion. However, as David Pepper has rightly observed, 'people will not change their values just through being "taught" different ones' (1984, p. 224). Pepper goes on: 'What, then, is the real way forward, if it is not to be solely or even largely through education? It must be through seeking *reform at the material base of society, concurrent with educational change*' (ibid., emphasis in the original). Quite – but how?

The answer to this question might just turn on initially sidestepping it and asking instead: *who* is best placed to bring about social change? A central characteristic of Green political theory is that it has never consistently asked that question, principally because the answer is held to be obvious: everyone. The general political-ecological position that the environmental crisis will eventually be suffered by everybody on the planet, and that therefore the ideology's appeal is universal, has been perceived as a source of strength for the Green movement. What could be better, from the point of view of advertising an idea, than to be able to claim that failure to embrace it might result in a global catastrophe that would leave no one untouched? From the present point of view this may be the movement's basic strategic political error because the universalist appeal is, properly speaking, Utopian. It is simply untrue to say that, given present conditions, it is in everybody's interest to bring about a sustainable and egalitarian society. A significant and influential proportion of society, for example, has a material interest in prolonging the environmental crisis because there is money to be made from administering it. It is Utopian to consider these people to be a part of the engine for profound social change.

Perhaps the most sophisticated expression of the universalist approach comes from Rudolf Bahro:

> If proceeding from these assumptions we are seeking a hegemonic project and want to keep to the level of the overall interest of humanity – which is what Marx had in mind with the world-historic mission of the proletariat – we must go beyond Marx's own concept and direct ourselves to a more general subject than the western working-class of today. Like the utopian socialists and communists who Marx sought to dispense with, we must once again take the species interest as our fundamental point of reference. (1982, p. 65)

Bahro's point here, couched in language expressive of his Marxist background, is that the social subject to which we must look in order to bring about change is not this or that social class but the whole human race. Again, he writes that 'From all appearances . . . the organising factors which can bring the alternative forces together and give then a social co-ordination (as must be desired) will in future not be any particular class interest, but rather a long-term human interest' (ibid., p. 115).

[153]

As I pointed out earlier, he can argue this because it appears transparent that the threatened environmental crisis will not discriminate between classes – the catastrophe, if it is to come, will be visited upon everybody. While this may be true in the long run, it is not necessarily the best point from which to plan immediate political strategy.

In many respects, for instance, one can already see that environmental degradation is not suffered by everyone equally. Organic foods as an alternative to chemical-dosed products, for example, are widely available in principle but their relative expense prevents them being accessible to all. It is not simply a question of education, then, but of money too. Similarly, if one considers the built environment, money makes available green spaces into which to retreat, and satisfying the primal call of the wilderness is an option presently open only to a very few.

More generally, it is simply not in the immediate interests of everybody to usher in a sustainable society. *The Limits to Growth* report remarks that, 'The majority of the world's people are concerned with matters that affect only family or friends over a short period of time. Others look farther ahead in time or over a larger area – a city or a nation. Only a very few people have a global perspective that extends far into the future' (Meadows *et al.*, 1974, p. 19). This captures the problem of persuasion with which the Green movement is confronted. Somehow people are required to begin to think in global terms and with respect to events that might or might not occur generations hence. 'Only a very few people' think like that, and they are precisely the people who already live in sustainable communities, refuse to use chemical pesticides in the garden, and flush the toilet only when they really have to. If these people constitute a vanguard, it is hard at present to see how they are going to drag large numbers of people with them. In the light of this, class theory has it that the Green movement must abandon its Utopian, universalistic strategy, and instead identify and organize a group of people in society whose *immediate* interests lie in living the Green life, with all that that implies.

[154]

With respect to everything that has been said so far about Green strategies for political change, it is interesting to look at the critique that Marx made of the Utopian socialists of the early nineteenth century (without jumping to the conclusion that this endorses everything Marx had to say, or comprises an embryonic Marxist critique of ecologism as a whole). This is what he said of them:

> They want to improve the condition of every member of society, even that of the most favoured. Hence they habitually appeal to society at large, without distinction of class; nay, by preference, to the ruling class. For how can people, when once they understand their system, fail to see in it the best possible plan of the best possible state of society? Hence they reject all political, and especially revolutionary, action; they wish to attain their ends by peaceful means, and endeavour, by small experiments, necessarily doomed to failure, and by the force of example, to pave the way for the new social gospel. (From *The Manifesto of the Communist Party* [1848], in Feuer, 1976, p. 79)

Word for word, these comments literally describe present Green, as well as the Utopian socialist, approach to political change. Marx makes two principal criticisms here, each of which contributes to his characterization of the type of socialism to which he refers as 'Utopian'. First, that Utopian socialism's appeal was counter-productive: it was objectively impossible to expect all classes to usher in socialism. Second, that its strategy of change through 'small experiments' and 'force of example' was an unfounded attempt to change *people* without changing the *conditions* in which they lived and worked.

Both of these criticisms of Utopian political strategy are relevant to the contemporary Green movement. The 'small experimental' nature of much of the movement's practice was made clear above. From the CAT in Wales, through any number of pesticide-free vegetable plots, to the New Age community at Findhorn, Scotland, the practice of much Green politics takes the form of a series of 'small experiments'. Marx, of course, made clear his recognition of the political value of the

Utopian socialists' enterprises for calling into question the accepted truths of early nineteenth-century European society, and any critique of Green Utopianism must do the same for the initiatives mentioned above.

It is well known that Marx's solution to the problem posed by the false universal appeal of the Utopian socialists was to recommend the identification and formation of a class in society (given the right historical conditions) whose prime interest lay in changing that society. This is how he put it in his *Toward a Critique of Hegel's Philosophy of Right* of 1844:

> Where is there, then, a *real* possibility of emancipation in Germany? This is our reply. A class must be formed which has *radical chains*, a class in civil society which is not a class of civil society, a class which is the dissolution of all classes, a sphere of society which has a universal character because its sufferings are universal, and which does not claim a *particular redress* because the wrong which is done to it is not a *particular wrong*, but *wrong in general*. There must be formed a sphere of society which claims no traditional status but only a human status, a sphere which is not opposed to particular consequences but is totally opposed to the assumptions of the German political system, a sphere which finally cannot emancipate itself without therefore emancipating all those other spheres, which is, in short, a *total loss* of humanity and which can only redeem itself by a *total redemption of humanity*. (In Bottomore and Rubel, 1984, p. 190)

According to Marx, then, the basic characteristics of the 'sphere of society' (or 'class') capable of bringing about profound social change were as follows: first, it had to have 'radical chains', such that, second, its emancipation would involve the general emancipation of humanity; and third, it had to be opposed not just to the 'particular consequences' of a political system but to its general 'assumptions'. For Marx, of course, this class with a universal historical mission was the proletariat. It is not novel to point out that the proletariat has not proved to be the class that Marx thought it was: its claims were not so radical that it questioned the assumptions of the political system, and its emancipation (while anyway only partial and material) has not led to the emancipation of humanity.

We are left, then, with a critique of Utopian (in Marx's rather specialized sense) political strategies, and how he considers it possible to transcend them. I shall discuss what might be the implications for the Green movement of Marx's critique of Utopian socialism a little further on, but first one or two words need to be said about the style of his project, and the difficulties anyone might have adapting it. There is considerable scepticism today among intellectuals on the left with respect not only to the faith that used to be placed in the working class as an agent for social change, but also to the whole notion of 'agents' of this type.

On what might very loosely be termed a post-modern reading, the search for a historical agent on which to found political change and which, moreover, is charged with saving not only itself but humanity as a whole is a universalistic project unwarranted by what we know of the world and how we know it. From this perspective, the universalizing project can only end in violence as its aims and intentions are necessarily frustrated, and as it seeks to recuperate itself by force. As Zygmunt Bauman has written: 'The typically post-modern view of the world is, in principle, one of an unlimited number of models of order, each one generated by a relatively autonomous set of practices', and, 'If, from the modern point of view, relativism of knowledge was a problem to be struggled against and eventually overcome in theory and in practice, from the post-modern point of view relativity of knowledge (that is, its "embeddedness" in its own communally supporting tradition) is a lasting feature of the world' (1987, p. 4). It is this relativity that disqualifies the search for totalizing truth or universalizing political ambitions.

Marx, of course, worked in a period that operated on different assumptions and in which, 'Like the knowledge they produce, intellectuals are not bound by localized, communal traditions. They are, together with their knowledge, extraterritorial' (ibid., p. 5). Hence, without the merest hint of self-conscious embarrassment, Marx is able to posit a class that will bring about 'the total redemption of humanity'. His framework is clearly modern as opposed to post-modern, and he fulfils (to employ the metaphors that comprise the felicitous title of Bauman's book) the intellectual's legislator, rather than interpreter, role. It seems that from a post-modern perspective any search for an agent for social change will be characterized as unwarranted (and ultimately violent) legislation, as is made clear in Bauman's sardonic observation: 'the present-day general intellectuals (or rather, the part of this category still faithful to the traditional, legislative definition of their role) are in Alvin Gouldner's famous phrase "shopping for an historical agent" again' (ibid., p. 177).

The reason for this short detour into post-modernity is that its critique of totalizing political aspirations must be taken seriously. In many respects, indeed, the Green strategies for change that I described earlier respond to post-modern celebrations of difference, diversity, unfoundedness and humility. The point might be made, though, that this has changed nothing – in Porritt's phrase already quoted it 'has not brought about the kind of fundamental shift that one might have expected'. The second point I would make is that it would be foolish and unwarranted for class theorists to make any universalistic claims for any agent they might identify. Whoever they think most likely to promote fundamental changes in society cannot be seen as paving the way for the salvation of humanity. Their project takes seriously Marx's criticism of Utopian socialism and uses it to expose the Utopian nature of current Green strategies for social change, and identifies a group of people whose immediate concerns connect with the movement's ultimate aims. In this sense it is claimed that it would be useful for the movement to take seriously the identification of an agent for Green change, but class theorists of such change ought to go no further than that.

We have already established that Green ideologues are typically averse to class theories of politics because they believe them divisively to undermine the Green universal appeal. There has, though, been some discussion of the general issue of agents for change in Green literature. Two suggestions can briefly be followed up: that of the middle class as the instigators of change, and the potentially central role of the 'new social movements', such as feminism, the peace movement, gays and so on.

Jonathon Porritt presents a classic formulation of the first position:

> one must of course acknowledge that the post-industrial revolution is likely to be pioneered by middle-class people. The reasons are simple: such people not only have more chance of working out where their own genuine self-interest lies, but they also have the flexibility and security to act upon such insights. (1986, p. 116)

Much depends here on just what one understands by 'pioneer'. If Porritt means simply the questioning of current social and political practices and the presentation of alternatives, then the middle class clearly has a central role to play. If, however, he sees the middle class as the engine of actual social change then he has to confront the issue of colonization referred to several times above. The middle classes are deeply implicated in present political practices, and in most respects their 'self-interest' as they perceive it lies in preserving them. Moreover, there is little sign of them being persuaded that their 'genuine' self-interest (as advertised by Green ideologues) lies in founding a sustainable society.

A further problem with Porritt's thesis is that it seems to fly in the face of one of his own central maxims. He writes, 'I do not believe that the majority of people will change until they believe it is in their own interests to do so . . . A reinterpretation of enlightened self-interest is therefore the key to any radical transformation' (ibid., p. 117). This is a reasonable position, but the conclusion that the middle class will therefore be the pioneers contradicts one of Porritt's earlier observations:

one thing is clear: even if we continue to think in terms of working class and middle class, it is not the latter that has the most to worry about in terms of the current crisis. It is the middle classes that have the flexibility to weather traumatic shifts in social and economic patterns; by and large, they are not the ones to suffer most from mindless jobs, dangerous working conditions, a filthy, polluted environment, shattered communities, the exploitation of mass culture, the inhumanity of bureaucrats and the mendacity of politicians. (ibid., p. 116)

On this reading, and taking into account Porritt's self-interest thesis, it is the working class and not the middle class whose interest lies in shifting away from present social practices. Porritt's conclusion in favour of the latter class, despite his own evidence, can be explained only by inserting him into the liberal tradition to which he belongs, and which has always proclaimed the middle classes as the agents of change.

It is this, too, that leads him to make optimistic remarks about 'the role of small businesses' under the general heading 'the agents of change' (ibid., p. 139). He goes on: 'In the kind of long-term economy that we envisage, small businesses would not just be a useful adjunct to the world of corporate big business: they would be the mainstay of all economic activity' (ibid.). The problem with the notion of small businesses as agents of change is that their success, and even survival, depends on their producing and reproducing the products and values demanded by the system within which they operate. In the name of efficiency, such businesses may 'have to' cut the workforce, deunionize it, hire temporary labour with no security, and provide poor conditions of work. There is no guarantee whatsoever that small businesses, far from acting as agents for social change, will not rather be vehicles for the reproduction of the system that they seek to overcome. Indeed, in the absence of any strategy for disengaging from the system, the latter is far more likely to be the case.

Beyond the middle class, one sometimes reads that the 'new social movements' represent new forms of political activity that anticipate new forms of society. Fritjof Capra, for example, writes of a 'winning majority' of 'environmentalists, feminists, ethnic minorities etc.', and then that 'the new coalitions should be able to turn the paradigm shift into political reality' (1983, p. 465). More explicitly, Murray Bookchin refers to 'the new classes' and argues that they are 'united more by cultural ties than economic ones: ethnics, women, countercultural people, environmentalists, the aged, the déclassé, unemployables or unemployed, the "ghetto" people' (1986, p. 152).

Similarly Jurgen Habermas, who is of course not a representative of the Green movement itself, has theorized a 'new politics' centring on 'the peace movement, the anti-nuclear and environmental movement, minority liberation movements, the movement for alternative lifestyles, the tax protest movement, religious fundamentalist protest groups and, finally, the women's movement' (Roderick, 1986, p. 136). Habermas goes on to make an important distinction that helps us to make some sense of the social pot-pourri offered up by himself, Capra and Bookchin. He argues that not all of these groups have the same emancipatory potential, and suggests that we distinguish between those that seek 'particularistic' change and 'those that seek fundamental change from a universalistic viewpoint' (ibid.). This ought to remind us of the quotation from Marx cited earlier in which he argued that the source of social change must be found in 'a sphere which is not opposed to particular consequences but is totally opposed to the assumptions of the German political system'. 'For Habermas,' continues Roderick, 'at the present time only the women's movement belongs to this latter category to the extent that it seeks not only a formal equality, but also a fundamental change in the social structure and in real concrete life situation' (ibid.).

This is a very important observation, particularly in the context of the most typical critique of social movements as agents for social change: i.e. that they have no common interest and therefore cannot act coherently. As Boris Frankel has written, for example, 'women, environmentalists, peace activists, gays, etc., do not have a ready-formed identity as a social movement' (1987, p. 235). This is undoubtedly true, but

[161]

with reference to Habermas' distinction it is hardly important. The crucial project would be not to manufacture an identity between heterogeneous groups, but to identify that group (or those groups) whose project most profoundly questions the presuppositions on which present social practices depend. Only such a group can already be in a sufficiently 'disengaged' position to resist the attempts at colonization by the system that it seeks to overcome, and even then, of course, success is by no means guaranteed.

The point of all this is to suggest that a possible strategy for the Green movement would be to identify and foment a group in society that is not only relatively 'disengaged' from it, but that also is already inclined towards the foundations of sustainable living. This will be the agent for Green change, and in the spirit of experiment I can now sketch what it might look like, beginning with a cursory Green materialist analysis of the situation that is producing it.

The Green movement will certainly want to argue that the production process is threatened by a shortage of material – that is precisely the point of its founding its ideology in the concept of a finite earth. If this is correct, then production itself will become ever more expensive (even allowing for temporary technological substitutes/solutions), and the capital required for investment in the process will become ever harder to find. There are two likely responses to this: first, the reduction of the costs of production in ways that will compensate for the increased cost of scarce materials; and second, the encouragement of increased consumption to generate more capital. A serious Green materialist analysis would of course need extensive empirical work to back up these claims.

The point in our context, though, is that the first strategy may come into conflict with the second and generate social tensions (and a social class) that cannot be satisfied within the current scheme of production and consumption. For instance, one of the ways in which the costs of production in the metropolitan countries can be reduced is by employing cheaper labour in other parts of the world. This, naturally, has the effect of increasing unemployment in the metropolitan countries. In turn, the number of people who are marginalized from the second response referred to above – that of encouraging increased consumption – increases. From their perspective, the system is characterized by its failure to fulfil the expectations it generates.

This characteristic is, of course, not new to the general history of the present mode of production, but Greens might argue that what is new to our particular period is that the external limits imposed by the earth circumscribe that system's room for manoeuvre. There is less and less space within which *both* to produce *and* to fulfil the expectations of consumption that the system generates. In other words, it might be argued from a Green perspective that the external limits imposed on the production process by the Earth itself are beginning to shape a class that is more or less permanently marginalized from the process of consumption. From this point of view it is *the distance from the process of consumption and the degree of permanence of this isolation that currently determine the capacity of any given group in society for Green social change.*

One (but only one) obvious group in contemporary society fits such a description and has been advanced (particularly by André Gorz) as an agent for change – the unemployed. The demands of this class are potentially radical: it will not seek higher wages, for it has no employment; it will not seek better working conditions because it has none to begin with; it will not ask for longer holidays because it is permanently on holiday (at least while not working in the underground economy); and it will not strike because it has no labour to withdraw. Lastly, because its problems are both caused by the present unsustainable economic system and insoluble within it, it would not press for a change in the ownership of the means of production, but would see that its interests lie in pressing for a change in the means of production themselves, towards a system that is sustainable.

In Marx's terms this class has 'radical chains' and is, as he went on to say, 'a class in civil society which is not a class of civil society'. In other words it is a class whose daily life sets it apart from all other classes of society. It is a class that does not buy anything and therefore calls into question the production process that fills the shop windows. In this sense it is a class that is opposed not just to the 'particular consequences' of this particular system, but to its general 'assumptions'. It is therefore so sufficiently 'disengaged' that it might hope to surmount the problems of colonization and recolonization that we saw dogging the parliamentary, lifestyle and community strategies for change.

At this stage we should recall the general thesis (a thesis that, once again, included the unemployed but does not exclusively relate to them) that it is 'the distance from the process of consumption and the degree of permanence of this isolation that currently determine the capacity of any given group in society for Green social change', and report the echoes of this thought that have already appeared in the Green literature.

Rudolf Bahro, for instance, has written that,

> More and more people are either excluded, marginalised, dismissed, or directly motivated to drop out, with either all or part of their energies. This gives rise by necessity to a strategy . . . that combines two elements: a gradually spreading *refusal* and a deliberate *obstruction*. This is not meant as a new discovery, I simply want to draw attention to what is necessary and deliberate in it. (1982, p. 154)

Bahro's notion of people 'dropping out' is the analogue of Marx's class that is 'in' civil society without being 'of' it, and this might be a defining characteristic of any group that hopes to be successful in challenging accepted norms and practices. Joe Weston seems to be pointing towards something similar when he argues that 'It is here, among the disenfranchised, that campaigning social environmentalism has its future' (1986, p. 154).

Another clear expression of this type of thinking comes, as I have already suggested, from André Gorz. In *Paths to Paradise* he wrote: 'the mass of disaffected non-workers is the *possible* social subject of the struggle for work-sharing, generalised reduction of work-time, gradual abolition of waged work by the expansion of autoproduction, and for a living income for all' (1985, p. 35). Gorz's recognition of the need for a social subject for political action and his identification of a 'new "non-class of post-industrial neo-proletarians" ' (Frankel, 1987, p. 210) as such a subject square with the general model described above (although Gorz's recommendations of autoproduction and reduced work-time are not, in my estimation, Green recommendations). Frankel goes on to explain the reasons behind Gorz's position: 'In not identifying with the production of waste, destruction and meaningless work to fill in time, the "non-class of neo-proletarians" are the only ones, Gorz believes, who will break through the "accumulation ethic" of "productivism" and bring into being the post-industrial society' (ibid., p. 211). This emphasizes the point that the radicalization of political consciousness can in principle occur in anyone, but that radical political change can be brought about only by those whose lived experience already demands it of them and makes it possible.

Gorz stresses that this lived experience is already one of segregation, not so much in opposition to present forms of living, as alongside and parallel to them:

Segregation of people for whom there is no permanent, full-time work is the common characteristic . . . How authoritarian this segregation will be depends on the political form and traditions of individual regimes: apartheid, gulags, compulsory paramilitary service; shanty-towns and North-American style urban ghettos, crowding together people who are mostly unemployed; or gangs of unemployed youth, subsidised eternal students and endless apprenticeships, temporary, holiday and seasonal workers etc.

In every case, the unemployed are *socially marginalised*, even when they are the majority (as in South Africa or some North American cities). They are deemed to be socially inferior and inadequate and effectively denied all social participation and activity. They remain outcasts and objects of resentment, begrudged whatever charity society grants them. (1985, p. 36)

In this respect, Gorz's 'neo-proletariat' does not 'identify the capitalist class as the dominant class to be overthrown' (Frankel, 1987, p. 212), but is marginalized even from that socialistic form of thinking. This is a class not in opposition, but in exclusion.

Nor should we be led to think that this class exists only in the metropolitan countries. In a speech in Caracas in 1981, Rudolf Bahro referred to what Arnold Toynbee called 'the external proletariat' and translated it, in general terms, into those who 'are not yet "really subsumed", i.e. the majority of the population who are marginalised to varying degrees and in varying ways' (1982, pp. 128–9). He continued: 'it may well be worthwhile to investigate the connection between the immediate interests of the marginalised sections (and these are growing now also in the metropolises, if on a different scale) and the general interest of a humanity which has reached the earth's limits with its industrial capitalist expansion' (ibid., p. 129).

Bahro is here pointing towards a social subject with similar characteristics to those that I have described (marginalization from the process of production and consumption), but situates it in the so-called Third World. This serves to emphasize the international character of the crisis and the shared interests of the 'metropolitan' and 'peripheral' marginalized, and provides the Green movement with an instance of, and practice for, its slogan: 'act locally, think globally.' Such a perspective also begins to give concrete content to Jeremy Seabrook's suggestion that 'the most urgent task is to show how and why the poor would be the chief beneficiaries of Green politics' (1988, p. 166). That is certainly not the way Green politics is presently conceived and I agree with Seabrook that, in the long run, 'Nothing could be more damaging to the Green cause than the perception that it is supported by privileged people who have enough for their own needs, and are now eager to limit the access of the poor to those benefits of industrial society which they themselves enjoy' (ibid., pp. 165–6).

[166]

Returning to Gorz, Boris Frankel makes three principal criticisms of his position, all of which can be only summarily addressed in the space available here. The first is the observation that 'High unemployment rates, temporary work and marginalized existences have characterized earlier generations and not just the new "neo-proletariat" ' (1987, p. 212). This may be true, but I have already indicated that from a Green perspective these negative aspects are due not solely to the demands of capital accumulation, but also to the likely increasing costs of production caused by maximizing unsustainable extraction in the context of a finite Earth. In other words, it has always been possible for capitalism and 'actually existing socialism' to promise employment and unmarginalized existences within their current systems. If the Green analysis of the consequences of our operating in a finite context is correct, then this promise no longer holds. Gorz's 'neo-proletariat' thus differs from the industrial proletariat in being – in principle – less open to co-option and colonization than its traditional counterpart.

This point also bears on Frankel's second criticism of Gorz, which is that 'many of the "neo-proletariat" . . . do feel guilty about being unemployed, do still identify with waste consumption and the work ethic, and are not mainly oriented to an alternative vision of autonomous free time' (ibid.). In other words, Frankel feels that marginalization from the process of consumption does not necessarily involve rejection of the entire political and economic system: it might just as easily result in an increased desire to become a part of it.

This appears to be a persuasive point, but I think that two responses might be made to it. First, there is the actual and objective existence of a number of people (drawn generally from what are traditionally defined as the middle classes) who have voluntarily decided on non-participation in consumption. Their particular lifestyles vary, but the common factor is a willingness (indeed, a desire) to live with less, or, as the Green movement would have it, to 'live lightly on the earth'. This, though, is a small proportion of the general population, and its

[167]

effect in terms of socio-political change can only be minimal, or 'small experimental', as Marx might have it.

Much more numerous and important are the tens of millions (in Western Europe alone) whose marginalization from the process of consumption might be argued to be structural and therefore insoluble within the current scheme of things. From a Green perspective, it is structural because the limits imposed by the Earth on the production process and the accumulation of capital make it impossible for this marginalized class ever to have access to the system's material benefits. Rudolf Bahro has observed that, 'So far in history the subordinate classes have essentially always wanted, in the last instance, what the privileged classes already possessed. Their habits are governed by what is in the shop windows which they press their noses against' (1982, p. 49). The point is that the Green movement could make the marginalized class aware that this habit has no future, and that its interests lie in a different form of society rather than immersion in the present one. Gorz's 'neo-proletariat', then, need not subscribe to current practices of production and consumption, but a precondition for it not doing so is an understanding that such practices actually reproduce, rather than alleviate, its marginalization. It is this recognition that Frankel's second criticism of Gorz misses.

His third criticism is that 'Gorz has exaggerated the number of people suffering from "neo-proletarian" symptoms' (Frankel, 1987, p. 213). The thinking here is that there are simply not enough 'neo-proletarians' to effect any radical social change. Much depends here on how we are to define member-ship of the class in the first place: confining it to the officially unemployed is the easiest way of assigning it a minority status. The number can be increased significantly by including all those in temporary or seasonal employment, and those who have found work in 'advanced industrial countries' over the past few years by accepting low wages, poor conditions, and geo-graphical displacement. The point of doing this is to illustrate that unemployment is only one form of marginalization from the process of consumption, that this latter is the crucial general characteristic of any social group likely to bring about political change, and that old age pensioners (who are due to number some 20% of the population in Britain by the year 2000) are as much members of this group as, say, the seasonally unemployed. It may even be, as Sara Parkin has suggested, that women and children constitute the most likely 'sustainable majority' in this context (in Dodds, 1988, p. 170). A further point is that if the maximization of production remains the goal of most societies, and if the Green analysis of a resulting deepening crisis of sustainability is correct, then the number of people marginalized from consumption can only, in the long term, increase. These are some possible preliminary responses to Frankel's third criticism of the 'neo-proletariat' thesis.

Central difficulties with the class-based strategy for Green change remain, however. Even assuming that the class has been formed, one is left with the problem of how it is going to act. Is it, for example, envisaged as some sort of revolutionary political subject? If so, then the class is confronted with a series of classic problems: the stability of current political systems (in the West at least), the issue of revolutionary organization, and (particularly difficult for non-violent Greens) waging the revolutionary struggle.

If, on the other hand, reformist strategies are chosen and the class operates through pressure groups or a parliamentary party then all of the dilemmas and difficulties referred to in the first part of this chapter resurface: how far should compromise be taken?, how should elections be contested?, is election a realistic possibility anyway? Intermediate strategies do present themselves, such as building up Green communities through the local money schemes described earlier (perhaps focussed on unemployment centres), but all thoughts of Green class action seem vitiated by the fact that no such class is presently in sight.

Conclusion

Discussion of any aspect of Green politics is always dogged by the necessity to distinguish between its dark-green and light-

[169]

green, or environmental, manifestations. The issue of Green social change is no exception. From a light-green point of view, for instance, the reflections which took place under the heading 'class' will probably seem superfluous. It appears self-evident that a parliamentary presence, or pressure through the lobby system can bring about a cleaner, more sustainable environment. It appears self-evident that we can lead more environment-friendly lives by buying the right things and refusing to buy the wrong ones. It also appears self-evident that sustainable communities are vital as sources of inspiration for the rest of us to live more lightly on the earth.

But all of these strategies must be measured in terms of the Green critique of present practices developed in Chapter 3, and the kind of life it is suggested we need to lead to overcome them. Bringing about that kind of sustainable society is an infinitely more difficult task than simply putting environmentalism on the political agenda. So far, that is what the strategies adopted have done, and taking Green politics seriously – rather than some attentuated environmentalist version of it – might involve a move beyond those strategies.

The universalist appeal has done the job required of it, probably more effectively than anyone dared hope. There can be no doubt that environmentalism will now find its way into all political party manifestos and that people will be ever more inclined to recycle their newspapers and bottles. Up to now the Green movement would have been content with this achievement. The present question is whether it remains serious about a Green and sustainable life for all, beyond environmentalism. If so, then its current political strategies may be found wanting.

CHAPTER 5

Ecologism, socialism and feminism

Left-wing ideology has not disputed the size and ingredients of the economic cake, arguing merely over how it should be sliced up. It shows no signs of recognizing that our problems start with the quantity and quality of the productive forces themselves. (Irvine and Ponton, 1988, p. 142)

Ecology is universally defined as the study of the balance and interrelationship of all life on earth. The motivating force behind feminism is the expression of the feminine principle. As the essential impulse of the feminine principle is the striving towards balance and interrelationship, it follows that feminism and ecology are inextricably connected. (Stephanie Leland, 1983, p. 72)

Ecologism can profitably be compared and contrasted with any one of a number of political–ideological positions. Although little substantial work has yet been done on this, some obvious lines of exploration are already opening up. Students of ecologism often remark, for example, upon the similarities in prescription between the kinds of communities that anarchists most normally describe and the picture of the sustainable society presented in Chapter 3. They will also comment on the conservatism that seems implicit in the ecologist's belief that there are natural limits to what we can do, and natural signs as to how we should live. Good politics, from this point of view, is a matter of adapting ourselves to a grand design rather than doing the designing ourselves. Then there is the liberal rationalism that produced natural rights and, later, human

[171]

rights, and which has been seen by many in the Green movement as the best way to generate a right for the environment and a consequent moral obligation for us to treat it with respect.

I could, in this chapter, be writing on any of these themes, and some more besides. But I have chosen to use the space available to consider two ideologies that have been substantially affected (some would say infected) by contact with the political ideology of ecologism. By this I mean that their engagement with ecologism has involved the possibility of calling into question, and thus reinterpreting, some of their basic tenets. The two ideologies in question are socialism and feminism.

On the face of it, the Green movement could hardly have appeared on the political scene at a worse moment from the point of view of socialism. In its actually existing form, from China and the Soviet Union through its various Euro-communist disguises to the parties of social democracy, socialism is under severe pressure. Its practices are still associated with bureaucratic management and centralism, and its basic principles, such as equality and community, have been pretty successfully presented recently as threats to the individual liberty that has been enthroned as the touchstone of political progress. Where 'socialist' governments still exist, such as in Australia or Spain, their policies are often hard to tell apart from those of their conservative opponents, and the same seems to go for socialism in opposition.

In this context of an assault by the right, the last thing socialism needed, so the argument goes, was a challenge to its hegemony on the left-hand side of the political spectrum. Early responses to the environmental movement from the socialist left were certainly hostile and often focused on its middle-class nature, either so as to illustrate its marginal relevance to the working class in particular and thus to socialism in general, or, more aggressively, to cast it in the role of a positive distraction from the fundamental battles still to be fought between capital and labour. Either way, the nascent Green movement was generally presented as a blip on the screen of radical politics, which would, probably, soon disappear and which, certainly, had nothing to say to the left that was worth listening to.

Reactions, though, have varied from country to country. In West Germany, where the Greens' leftist orientation has been marked from the beginning, the debate between 'red' and 'green' that has now begun elsewhere hardly needed to be initiated explicitly because it was present at the start. More accurately, those on the left in Germany who were comfortable in Green company were those with a decentralist and 'Utopian' socialist heritage – precisely the heritage that has been 'rediscovered' by those socialists outside Germany who have taken the ecological challenge seriously. The result in West Germany has been a flood of thinking around the issue of eco-socialism, while the wider ideological and institutional divide between red and green in Britain, for example, has taken some time to bridge.

But it is being bridged, and the outcome is a cross-fertilization of ideas and practices, which has the potential for sharpening the ecological critique and which may breathe new life into the socialist project. In the pages that follow I shall set out what I consider to be the principal socialist criticisms of Green politics, and then show the ways in which socialists sensitive to the ecological position have reinterpreted their own tradition so as to accommodate it. I do not, though, want to give the impression that, since the original leftist onslaught on environmental politics, dealings between the two sides have been characterized by a friendly exchange of mutually compatible and regenerative information. The debate continues to be acrimonious at times and often there is no debate at all. Jonathon Porritt and Nicholas Winner, for example, refer to David Pepper's presentation of the Green movement as 'deeply conservative' and 'reactionary' and as 'just so much angry sputtering from worn-out ideologues who have long since lost touch with the real world' (1988, p. 256). Sandy Irvine and Alec Ponton of the British Green Party pointedly characterize socialism as 'fair shares in extinction' (1988, p. 142). Elsewhere though, and particularly in the work of Raymond Williams,

[173]

Boris Frankel and Peter Gould, great strides have been taken (on the socialist side at least) to come to terms with the Green perspective without abandoning original socialist impulses. It is with these contributions that this chapter is in part engaged.

While socialists have had to engage with ecologism, there has been no real sense in which this has involved a battle over the meaning of socialism itself. At most the engagement has produced a recuperation of subordinate traditions within socialism, but without elbowing other traditions out of the way altogether. Things are somewhat different, though, for feminism. There is combat between those feminists who subscribe to the type of feminism normally associated with Green politics – to be described later in the chapter – and those who consider that type of feminism to be a retrograde step in the struggle for women's liberation. In this sense the conversation between feminists in the Green context amounts to a debate about the direction of the movement itself.

We are familiar with the development of the women's movement from a general rights-based demand for social and political parity with men, through to the notion of the liberation of women as women based on the suspicion that equality with men in a man-created context might involve the suppression of valued characteristics actually or potentially possessed by women. In many respects, the feminism associated with Green politics subscribes to the second strategy, and in a way considered dangerous by those who seek to preserve and advance the gains made by following the first strategy. The danger is held to lie in the 'valued characteristics' ascribed to women by some Green feminists – characteristics such as a caring, nurturing nature and a readiness to reinvest emotion with the positive value removed from it by the male enthronement of rationality. These characteristics are often collected under the notion of the 'feminine principle' referred to in Stephanie Leland's quotation at the head of this chapter, and in numerous other spots throughout Green literature. Often, what is demanded is a balancing of 'male' and 'female' qualities,

[174]

beginning from the position that the former presently pre-
dominate and are deemed (wrongly) to be of greater value than
the latter.

It is easy to see why this kind of feminism is attractive to the
Green movement: the characteristics thus ascribed to women
are precisely those that ecologists would want us all to develop,
in respect of our dealings both with other people and with the
non-human natural world. And I am sure that it is just this that
makes other feminists suspicious of Green man's readiness to
adopt his sisters' perspective. Green man might well want to
care, nurture, be more emotional and practise the 'culture of the
hearth' (Simonon, 1983, p. 199); but in the meantime someone
has to get out into the public arena and proselytize, and, because
Green woman is at home caring and nurturing (she does it so
well), it had better be him. This debate constitutes the second
part of this chapter, but now I turn to the issue of socialism and
ecology and, first, the principal criticisms that socialists lay at
the ecologists' door.

Socialism and ecology

Capitalism or industrialism?

We know by now that one of the reasons the Green movement
considers itself to be 'beyond left and right' is because it believes
this traditional spectrum of opposition to be inscribed in a more
fundamental context of agreement: a 'super-ideology' called
'industrialism'. Greens 'stress the similarities between capitalist
and socialist countries' (Porritt and Winner, 1988, p. 256) in that
they are both held to believe that the needs of their respective
populations are best satisfied by maximizing economic growth.
The equating of capitalism with socialism engendered by the
identification of 'industrialism' is the aspect of Green thinking
most often attacked by its socialist critics, and Joe Weston's 'It
is time that greens accepted that it is capitalism rather than
industrialism *per se* which is at the heart of the problems they

[175]

address' (1986, p. 5) is a typical refrain. Rudolf Bahro made a similar remark when he was still a socialist:

> This common standpoint [between Greens and socialists] is a radical critique of capitalist industrialism. Many Greens may initially not think of capitalist industrialism but of the consequences of the industrial system in general. But in this respect they are misled. (1982, p. 24)

Socialists make remarks like this, in the first place, not because they don't agree with ecologists that environmental decay is upon us but because they argue that it is capitalism's use of industry to produce for profit and not for need, rather than 'industry' itself, that causes the problems. Greens will accept that the destruction of capitalism is indeed a necessary condition for restoring environmental integrity but do not see it as a sufficient condition, particularly when they point to actually existing socialist countries that have some of the worst environmental records in the entire world. Socialists respond by pointing out that none of these countries are socialistic in the sense they want to ascribe to the word, and that this is because they have developed the same 'form of demand for material goods' as the capitalist nations, in competition with them. In this sense 'capitalism permeates the whole globe' (Weston, 1986, p. 4), and as Bahro wrote: 'We have precisely learned that the Russian revolution did not manage to break with the capitalist horizon of *development of productive forces*. We have seen how right round the globe it is one and the same technology that has triumphed' (1982, p. 131).

In this way, socialists sidestep the Green invitation to consider the environmental problems suffered by socialist countries and to draw the conclusion that there is little to choose between socialist and capitalist management of industry (from the environment's point of view). They then suggest that a truly socialist society would produce for need and not for profit, and that consideration of the environment would be integral to policy formation. However, in one important respect (from a socialist point of view) the issue is not over what a socialist society might or might not do, but that the Green refusal to recognize capitalism as the root of the problem renders ecology incapable of fighting its battles in the right places. If, from an environmental perspective, the socialist view of capitalism is correct, then ecologism's best way forward is to confront the capitalist manifestation of industrialism rather the many-headed hydra, industrialism itself.

Joe Weston reminds us that this would involve the restate-ment of traditional socialist principles and practices, on the basis that 'what we find is that behind virtually all environmental problems, both physical and social, is poverty' (1986, p. 4). Indeed, many socialists will analyse phenomena like deforesta-tion from just this point of view – the fundamental problem is much more one of inequitable land distribution (which produces the slash-and-burn farmers) and structural poverty (which produces periodic but highly damaging jungle gold rushes), than it is one of an insatiable and environmentally insensitive desire to eat hamburgers. From this point of view, environmentalist (or even ecologist) strategies will be found wanting: Weston suggests that, 'Saving hedgerows does not confront capitalism in the same way as do issues relating to poverty; poverty is, after all, of crucial importance to capitalism and has to be maintained in order to preserve the balance of power in market relationships' (ibid., p. 156). Poverty, then, is at the root of most environmental problems and a far-reaching redistribution of wealth is the solution. Crucially, an attack on poverty would constitute an attack on capitalism, and would therefore be a blow against the root cause of environmental decay.

The Green question now might be: why should a redistribu-tion of wealth bring about improvements in the environment? Much evidently turns on just what 'environment' one is talking about, and it is a socialist strategy with respect to ecologism to accuse it of too narrow a definition of the term, as I shall show below. It is probably true that radical redistributions of wealth would improve the sanitation, housing and food of millions of dispossessed poor both here and in the so-called third world, and that this would constitute a significant improvement in their environment. But it is hard to see how a redistribution of wealth on its own would address Green warnings about the unsustainability of present industrial practices. One can perfectly well imagine a world in which incomes between and within countries were more or less the same, but which still subscribed to the view that there were no limits to industrial growth. Indeed, this is precisely the world that the dominant themes of socialism have advertised since its inception, and it is the reason why Greens are wary of attacks on capitalism that have no ecological content. In this sense, Weston talks past the Green movement rather than to it when he says: 'The problems with which most people are now faced are not related to "nature" at all: they are related to poverty and the transfer of wealth and resources from the poor to an already wealthy minority of the Earth's population' (1986, p. 14).

So Weston's attempt to sensitize the Green movement to the capitalist problematic appears to lead him back into unreconstructed criticisms of capitalism (with which few in the Green movement ought to disagree) that pay little mind to the central Green question: why should socialism be any more concerned about sustainability than capitalism? The great value in his position, though, is that it forces ecologists to take capitalism seriously. The fact is that, while capitalism can absorb environmentalism and some people can get very rich out of it, the deeper Green programme constitutes a serious threat to both the social relations and productive practices typical of capitalism. At some stage ecologism, if it makes any progress at all, will have to confront capitalist institutions and could profitably take that confrontation seriously here and now. This might involve wedding classic socialist positions to demands for sustainability: Greens cannot ignore capitalism but neither is it enough (from their point of view) to change the relations of production without changing the character of production itself.

The 'end of ideology'

As I suggested in Chapter 1, some socialists have detected the nasty but familiar smell of the 'end of ideology' in the Green 'industrialism' thesis. For socialists there is no more important political battle to be fought than that between capital and labour, and any politics that claims to transcend this battle is regarded with suspicion. The idea that the interests of capital and labour have somehow converged amounts to a betrayal, from the socialist point of view, of the project to liberate labour from capital. The interests of capital and labour are not the same, yet the Green belief that both are inscribed in the super-ideology of industrialism makes it seem as though they are.

At root, proposes Joe Weston, the Green movement's mistake is to refuse a class analysis of society – it 'argues that traditional class divisions are at an end' (1986, p. 22), and uses the concept 'industrial society . . . to distinguish contemporary society from orthodox capitalism; it is not a neutral term' (ibid.). It is not neutral in the sense that it removes capitalism from the glare of criticism and thus contributes to its survival and reproduction. Similarly, the original 'end of ideology' thesis was accompanied by an analysis of how policies are formulated and social conflicts resolved, collected under the term 'pluralism'. Socialists have always considered this to be a dubious description, principally because the apparently democratic diversity and openness it implies serve to obscure capitalism's hierarchy of wealth and power, based on the domination of labour by capital.

From Weston's point of view it is no accident, therefore, that the Green movement's 'industrialism' thesis, kept company by the abandonment of a class analysis of society, also results in a political practice based around the pressure groups of pluralism. In this sense there is no difference between Daniel Bell and Jonathon Porritt, which is sadder for the latter than for the former given that Porritt is seeking fundamental change in society. In the first place, Porritt's attack on industrialism

[179]

prevents him from seeing that the real problem is capitalism; second, his failure to subscribe to a class analysis of society leads him to the dead-end of pressure group politics; and third – and probably most serious from a socialist point of view – not only is he not attacking capitalism as he should, but he is contributing to its survival by deflecting criticism from it.

Defining 'the environment'

It transpired above that Joe Weston's argument that a redistribution of wealth would help solve environmental problems was based upon an interpretation of 'environment' not usually associated with the Green movement. In his opinion, Greens have policed the word into meaning 'nature': 'the prime concern of the greens is indeed ecology and "nature", which means that other, far more immediate environmental problems are neglected' (1986, p. 2) and, more specifically, 'we have a central government which appoints a special "green Minister" to tackle ecological decline while the problems of poverty and street violence go unrecognized as environmental issues' (ibid., p. 4). In this context it is indulgent and irresponsible for the Green movement to concentrate its 'not inconsiderable resources upon protecting hedgerows, butterflies and bunny rabbits' (ibid., p. 12) while the day-to-day built environments of large numbers of people are in such urgent need of reconstruction.

Sections of the Green movement appear to have taken this kind of criticism on board – witness the Friends of the Earth's 'Cities for People' campaign – but there is still a sense in which Weston's critique speaks past the movement rather than to it. Greens have a very good reason for referring so often to the biospherical environment: they are concerned for its survival as a long-term supporter of human and non-human life. From this perspective Weston is right to ask Greens to reassess their understanding of 'the environment', but wrong to ask them to focus on inner-city environments if the recipes for them are not placed in the context of the search for a sustainable society.

[180]

Socialists (and others) will argue, in any case, that there is no such thing as 'nature' unmediated by human beings, and therefore no great difference between the urban environment and the environment created by farmed land or deforestation: social relations and the capitalist mode of production that underpins them 'produce' the environment. Green exhortations to 'protect' or 'conserve' the environment betray the unfounded impression that there is an 'untouched' nature alongside the bits already corrupted by human beings, and it is this untouched nature that receives the movement's greatest attention. Socialists will argue that an awareness of the social construction of the environment would have three effects: first, it would lead to a healthy widening of Green activity; second, it would promote an understanding of the capitalist roots of environmental decay – both in the countryside and in the cities; and third, it would improve the chances of the Green movement obtaining a mass following.

This last point needs some explanation. Joe Weston argues that the Green movement as presently constituted is an expression of the ennui of a particular section of the middle class – the professional, educated section. Green politics is 'an attempt to protect the values – rather than simply the economic privilege – of a social group which rejects the market-orientated politics of capitalism and the materialistic analysis made of it by Marxists' (ibid., p. 27). These values are reflected, partly, in the 'green' definitions of the environment most often advanced by the movement, referred to above. To the extent that this is 'a political perspective which is specific to a particular social group' (ibid., p. 28), and, moreover, a social group that is of limited size, no mass movement can be formed around it. On this reading ecologism will not progress beyond its minority, subordinate status until it speaks to the kinds of environmental problems suffered by masses of people. This it will never do, suggests Weston, unless it breaks out of its middle-class laager and recognizes that 'rather than conserving the environment in which most people now live, the inner city and the shanty town need destroying' (ibid., pp. 14–15).

Just how unique is *Green politics?*

So the Green movement in general considers itself to be above discussions about the relative merits of capitalism and socialism and is presented as having moved beyond these old debates towards something uniquely fresh and novel. Apart from disagreeing with the premise of that position and arguing that, far from transcending the battle, ecologists have settled down dangerously close to the capitalist camp, socialists will argue that much of the Green programme is at least as old as socialism itself. The tactical reason behind this move is clear: to take some of the shine off the attractive newness of ecologism and so recapture some of the ground lost to it in the arena of radical politics. In this context David Pepper quotes Jonathon Porritt: the 'dual [Green] emphasis on decentralization and internationalism is quite unique to the green perspective' and goes on to call Porritt's bluff by referring to 'a whole lineage of socialist and populist thinkers' who subscribed to the self-same principles – Kropotkin, Proudhon, Godwin, William Morris, Robert Owen and the Diggers and Levellers (in Weston, 1986, p. 117).

If this does enough to expose the selectivity of Porritt's political memory, then Martin Ryle goes further by suggesting that the Green movement *has* to borrow from pre-existing traditions to inform its programme. This is because, very importantly, 'ecological limits may limit political choices, but they do not determine them' (1988, p. 7). So the Green movement 'finds itself asking not just what kinds of social relations are ecologically viable, but what kinds are good' (ibid., p. 20). The point is that a sustainable society could take many forms; if sustainability were the only issue at stake then 'authoritarian post-capitalist' or 'barrack socialist' (ibid., p. 7) solutions could equally well fit the bill. The fact that the Green movement tends not to go for those options suggests that it will tap into traditional sources of objection to them, and will therefore clothe its arguments in long-existing drapery. In this respect Ryle finds ecology and socialism not too far apart. He

[182]

argues that 'The values of the Greens, their commitment to justice and liberty, cannot be adequately anchored in "ecology", but derive from a long tradition of progressive thought and struggle – liberal and libertarian and socialist' (ibid., p. 12). The substantive point is that:

> The political meanings attributed to 'social ecology' or 'the ecological paradigm' really derive from, and can only be discussed in terms of, traditions and debates (individualism versus collectivism, competition versus mutuality, authority and hierarchy versus liberty and equality) which long predate the emergence of ecology as a scientific discipline. (ibid.)

This seems to me to be absolutely right. In their efforts to stake out new and uncharted political territory, ecologists often too hastily disengage themselves from already existing traditions. Not only do they speak in terms of concepts that have been the stuff of political discussion for centuries but they fill out those concepts in very particular ways – often socialistic ways. Apart from the claim of novelty being disingenuous, it can also have the effect of marginalizing the Green movement from possible sources of support, and I take it that Ryle is pointing out common heritages precisely with a view to forms of united thought and action. One point that will emerge later in the chapter, though, is that in order to build such bridges Ryle has to be selective with respect to socialism's heritage – just as Pepper was, in a catholic sort of way, in selecting anarchists and Utopian socialists for his rebuff of Porritt, above.

Organization

Socialists – and others – argue that the Green decentralist programme is unrealistic for three principal reasons. First, not everything that we might reasonably expect from a Green society can be produced locally; second, dealing with the environmental problems that the Green movement has identified requires the kind of planning that can only be provided by

[183]

centralized political structures; and third, such structures are needed to organize the redistribution required by the Greens' egalitarian project. I suggest that Greens (or rather some of them, depending on what their picture of a sustainable society looks like) are perfectly able to accept these points within the framework provided by their maxim that no decision should be taken at a higher level that can be taken at a lower level.

With respect to the first issue Martin Ryle argues that it is not possible to make 'fridges, bicycles [or] kidney dialysis machines' in 'domestic enterprises or craft workshops' (1988, p. 23) – or at least certainly not to the standard required for the safe operating of complex equipment. Chinese experiences of decentralized production under Mao suggest that even relatively uncomplicated goods are hard to produce adequately.

Second, Ryle points out that 'ecological restructuring' as opposed to 'environmental protection through piecemeal legislation' (ibid., p. 63) will involve planning, and concludes that, although one might prefer to have no state:

> If one is honest about the objectives which an ecologically enlightened society would set for itself, it is difficult to avoid concluding that the state, as the agent of collective will, would have to take an active law-making and -enforcing role in imposing a range of environmental and resource constraints. (ibid., p. 60)

On this reading planning is essential if the Green programme is to be realized, and such planning can be devised and carried out only by centralized political structures. Ryle makes the interesting further point that, if it could be successfully argued that environmental problems can be relieved only by intervention, it might be possible more generally to turn the tables on the free-marketeers: 'the idea of an *ecological* transformation of the economy can itself play a part in renewing the legitimacy of political interventions in the market' (ibid., p. 66).

Boris Frankel adds that redistribution with a view to egalitarianism presupposes centralized structures too:

Until individuals and groups accept the unpalatable news that stateless, decentralized, moneyless, small-scale communes or other informal alternatives are not viable without the complex administrative and social structures necessary to guarantee democratic participation, civil rights and egalitarian co-ordination of economic resources, there is not much hope of strong coalitions between labour movements and new social movements. (1987, p. 270)

The Green movement might make two responses to these remarks. In the first place some of them will say that it is a caricature of their position to imply, as Ryle and Frankel do, that they seek entirely stateless societies. They will say that only the bioregionalists and the extreme commune theorists would subscribe to that, and that although they influence the movement's thinking it would be wrong to argue that their position is exhaustively representative of the movement's as a whole. This is not to say that the movement doesn't exhibit confusion on this score, and there are clearly problems associated with the programme of seizing central power and then giving it away again, but this is not the same as suggesting that the Green movement is innocent of the need to plan. Critics might still retort, in any case, that the Green sustainable society just is stateless and that members of the movement who claim otherwise are doing so precisely to avoid the sort of question that has been put to them.

Greens might put their same argument a different way. They can also say that, rather than pushing for the abolition of the centralized state, the movement is merely asking that the ground-rules for decision-making be changed. Presently the onus of justification is on those who would have decision-making locally based, and ecologists would like to see this reversed. In other words, the current norm is for decisions to be taken at high levels, while under a Green regime decisions would be taken at low levels unless it were expressly necessary for them to be taken higher up. In this context the kinds of decision and the types of production to which Frankel and Ryle

[185]

refer (income or resource distribution and kidney dialysis machines) are precisely those that would justifiably correspond to higher levels according to the Green maxim. In this sense the socialist critique of Green forms of organization enables us to clarify the Green movement's position rather than undermine it.

We have it, then, that socialists will often reject the Green 'industrialism' thesis and seek to locate the causes of environmental decay more specifically in the capitalist mode of production; that this may be accompanied by worries about the system-supportive nature of the Green movement in the guise of the 'end of ideology' thesis; that the 'environment' needs to be defined more widely so as to address the concerns of majorities, rather than minorities, of people; that ecologists ought to spend less time making unsustainable claims for originality, and more time recognizing common heritages and programmes; and that Green decentralist aspirations are at odds with the planning their programme presupposes. The answer to the question of how constructive these socialist comments on ecology are intended to be varies from writer to writer, and depends on the extent to which they have realigned themselves after confrontation with the basic ecological theses concerning limits to growth and so on. The nature of this realignment comes next.

Limits to growth

The most instructive test to carry out on would-be Green socialists is to see how far they have accepted the fundamental Green position that there are material limits to productive growth. Some have done so completely and in the process would appear significantly to have reassessed the content of their socialism. Rudolf Bahro, for example, commented when he was still a socialist that he found it 'quite atrocious that there are Marxists who contest the finite scope of the earth's exploitable crust' (1982, p. 60). We now know that Bahro's dwelling on thoughts like this led him to abandon socialism

[186]

entirely. Not so Joe Weston and Raymond Williams, but they would probably nevertheless agree with the following remarks:

> I do not believe that anyone can read the extensive literature on the ecology crisis without concluding that its impact will oblige us to make changes in production and consumption of a kind, and on a scale, which will entail a break with the life-styles and expectations that have become habitual in industrialized countries. (Ryle, 1988, p. 6)

Joe Weston certainly agrees, up to a point: 'it must be stressed that this rejection of green politics does not mean that we now believe that natural resources are infinite' (1986, p. 4) and adds that the left can learn from the Greens to call the project of 'perpetual industrial expansion' into question (ibid., p. 5). Raymond Williams, too, accepts the ecological position with respect to 'the central problem of this whole mode and version of production: an effective infinity of expansion in a physically finite world' (1986, p. 214) and suggests that 'the orthodox abstraction of indefinitely expanded production – its version of "growth" – has to be considered again, from the beginning' (ibid., p. 215).

Without explicitly wanting to do so, this reconsideration also seems to involve Williams in reconsidering socialism itself. He writes that 'any socialist should recognise' 'the certainty that many of the resources at their present levels of use are going to run out' (1986, n.d., p. 15), and that consequently socialists should rethink their traditional belief that the relief of poverty requires 'production, and more production' (ibid., p. 6). But then it turns out that this is not a traditional socialist belief after all, for Williams suggests that: 'We have to build on the socialist argument that productive growth, as such, is not the abolition of poverty' (ibid., p. 15). Williams seems to be saying both that socialism does hold the belief that the relief of poverty requires more production and, then, that it does not.

Of course socialists have always argued for an equitable

[187]

distribution of what is produced and in this sense Williams is consistent, but socialism has no dominant tradition of production itself being called into question, and this is what Williams is hinting at here. Certainly *Marxism Today*, for example, would consider his position to be heretical: 'the question of reindustrialisation and growth distinguishes the Ecology Party, and green politics generally, quite sharply from the Left' (in Porritt, 1984, p. 25). Similarly Frank Richards restates the classic left position when he writes that 'The number of people which can be supported by an area of land is not given by nature, but by the sort of society in which they are organised' (1989, p. 21).

Raymond Williams, then, appears above to be rereading socialism and when he refers to 'the pressure point on the whole existing capitalist mode of production' as 'the problem of resources' (1986, n.d., p. 16) he leaves us in no doubt. We will not find this kind of analysis of the weaknesses of capitalism in any of the dominant sources of socialist thought. To this degree, acceptance of the Green position that there are limits to productive growth can have considerable repercussions with respect to the content of the socialism espoused by socialists.

Reassessment of the socialist tradition

One of the repercussions that stands out is a rethinking of the socialist tradition itself, in the sense of a stressing of some aspects of it at the expense of others. Socialists who have come into sympathetic contact with ecologism without embracing it altogether have tended to try to claim that socialism has been saying the same thing all along. These are claims not merely of compatibility but of seniority, as socialists seek to defuse the ecological challenge.

Not surprisingly it is decentralist, non-bureaucratic, non-productivist socialism to which writers like Williams most often refer, and the Utopian socialists and William Morris are those usually resurrected as evidence for its existence. Thus Rudolf Bahro suggested that 'we shall scarcely come up against any elements that have not already emerged in the writings of one or other of the old socialists, including of course the utopians' (1982, p. 126). By 1984 he was saying: 'If pushed hard I couldn't deny that I am a utopian socialist because so many of the elements of utopian socialism appear in my commune perspective' (p. 235). Martin Ryle echoes this sentiment: 'utopian socialism would seem to be an obvious point of convergence between greens and socialists' (1988, p. 21), while Robin Cook of the Labour Party is more specific: 'the future of socialism may lie more with William Morris than with Herbert Morrison' (Gould, 1988, p. 163), as is Raymond Williams: 'The writer who began to unite these diverse traditions, in British social thought, was William Morris' (n.d., p. 9).

From the other side Jonathon Porritt accepts such genealogies too: 'My own personal points of familiarity and very close connection with the Left come from the early libertarian traditions, William Morris and so on, and from the anarchist tradition of left politics', and he adds a significant point: 'I think that form of decentralised socialism is something that has had a pretty rough time in socialist politics during the course of this century' (1984, p. 25).

What emerges from these exchanges is evidence for the selective way in which both socialists and ecologists refer to the socialist tradition. Usually, Porritt does not make the distinctions he makes above. He is keen to disassociate ecologism from socialism because he sees the latter as part of the old order, and so usually refers to it in its bureaucratic, productivist guise. To the extent that there is a decentralist tradition within socialism this is a disingenuous move, but it would be equally disingenuous for socialists to respond to the ecologists' challenge by arguing (suddenly) that William Morris is what real socialism is all about.

Sometimes socialists bend over too far backwards in their search for compatible characters. When David Pepper refers for example to a 'Kropotkin–Godwin–Owen' tradition (in Weston, 1986, p. 120), one wonders whether we're talking about socialism at all any more. At the very most there is only one socialist among those three, and, although Pepper does cover himself by positing an 'anarchist rather than centralist' form of socialism (ibid., p. 115), the adjective 'anarchist' has the effect of divesting socialism of much of the resonance usually attributed to it. But there is little to be gained from semantics. The important point is that claims for a convergence between socialism and ecology rest on the resurrection of a subordinate tradition within socialism. To this extent the question whether or not socialism and political ecology are compatible cannot be answered without first asking: 'what kind of socialism?', and in the end the answer will turn on whether the Utopian/William Morris tradition argues for a sustainable society in anything like a modern Green sense.

Autarky, and the working class

Two further Green political themes that recur in the socialist response deserve brief mention before moving on to think about the relationship between ecology and feminism. The first is autarky, and the second concerns the role of the working class in bringing about social change. We saw in Chapter 3 that ecologists favour some measure of autarky for a variety of reasons, and Boris Frankel (at least) is prepared to follow a similar path. From an eco-socialist point of view, Martin Ryle has argued that it would be beneficial for both the first and the third worlds, and that its principal advantage is that the alternative – 'collective development of new international structures' – would be hard to bring about (1988, p. 84). Three (significant) difficulties he identifies are: the likelihood of autarky fanning the flames of nationalism, the problems associated with disengaging from current patterns of inter-penetration, and the fact that trade can help to equalize inequalities of resources between nations.

In the same vein, Boris Frankel sees 'semi-autarchy' (1987, pp. 248–52) as a useful corrective to the 'powerful illusion' (held, he notes, by very many democratic socialists) of supranational solutions to the 'irrationality and conflict induced by imperialist and nationalist institutions and practices'. He sees such solutions as an 'anti-democratic nightmare', which would threaten 'indigenous local and national control over vital assets, resources, skills [and] technology'. Semi-autarky, on the other hand, would in principle both maximize the autonomy of local and national economies and help to avoid the 'narrow parochialism' that he (and Ryle, above) feel would be the result of 'full self-sufficiency'.

As far as the issue of class is concerned, we saw earlier in the chapter that socialists are wary of Green claims to have moved beyond the politics of class, but it is still the case that some of them who have come into contact with ecology have had to reassess the idea that the working class is the repository of progressive social change. At the technical Marxist level, for example, Rudolf Bahro was led (while still a socialist) to stop looking upon 'the actual working classes as if the proletariat with a world-historic mission was waiting in them for its time to arrive, as if their economic interests were accordingly the yardstick for social movements in general' (1982, p. 110). He later referred to the working class, from a global ecological standpoint, as 'the worst exploiting class in history'; while no self-respecting socialist I know would go so far, there has certainly been a tendency among some of them to drift towards the view that the 'new social movements' constitute the brightest hope for progressive change (see Chapter 4 for a discussion of the relative merits of 'movements' and 'class' in the context of social change). The idea that 'issues' might generate more political momentum than 'class' has been central to Green strategy from the outset and some eco-socialists seem prone to agree.

Concluding ecology and socialism

Under pressure from the Greens, some socialists will reassess the traditional goals of production and indiscriminate growth; they will seek to rescue subordinate strains in their political tradition and they may ponder the role of the working class in future political transformations. Greens themselves need to listen to the socialist critique and to think harder about the relationship between capitalism and environmental degradation, about just what 'the environment' is, and about the potential for social change implicit in the identification of a social subject. In the end, Martin Ryle is probably right to identify political ecology and socialism as engaged on a 'converging critique': they both see capitalism as wasteful of resources in terms of production and consumption, and they both criticize it for its inegalitarian outcomes (1988, p. 48). But the principal question is practical rather than theoretical: which of the two has the best strategy for bringing about an egalitarian sustainable society?

Ecofeminism

I suggested near the beginning of the chapter that if the debate between political ecology and socialism is best characterized as a debate *between* ways of thinking and acting, then the debate centred on ecofeminism is more accurately described as a debate *within* a way of thinking and acting. I shall try to show how this latter debate is a part of a general conversation within feminism as to the best way to proceed: whether to seek equality with men on terms substantially (but arguably) offered by men, or whether to focus on the differences between men and women and to seek to re-evaluate upwards the currently suppressed (supposed) characteristics of women. In general, ecofeminism subscribes to the second strategy but not, importantly, with a view to liberating women only, but also with a view to encouraging men to adopt 'womanly' ways of thinking and acting, thus promoting healthier relationships between people in general, and also between people (but especially men) and the environment.

Ecofeminism seems to be built around three principal sets of thoughts. In the first place, ecofeminists usually argue for the existence of values and ways of behaving that are primarily female in the sense of more fundamentally possessed by, or exhibited by, women rather than men. It doesn't seem to matter whether these characteristics are 'socially' or 'biologically' produced, although of course to the extent that ecofeminists would like to see men taking on these characteristics they have to believe it is possible for them to do so. In other words, they cannot argue that it is necessary to be a woman to have such characteristics, although they might suggest that men cannot know what they are unless they listen to women telling them. Associated with this belief is the idea that female values have, historically, been undervalued by patriarchy and that it is the ecofeminist's task to argue for their positive re-evaluation. Of course, if there are female values and ways of behaving then there are also male values and ways of behaving. In asking that female traits be re-evaluated upwards, ecofeminists do not necessarily demand that male traits be policed out of existence – rather they are likely to seek a balance of the two.

The second idea is that the domination of nature is related to the domination of women, and that the structures of domination and the reasons for it are similar in both cases: 'The identity and destiny of women and nature are merged', write Andrée Collard and Joyce Contrucci (1988, p. 137). The third idea – related to and tying up the first two – is that women are closer than men to nature and are therefore potentially in the vanguard as far as developing sustainable ways of relating to the environment is concerned. I shall expand on these three notions and show how some feminists have balked at the ecofeminist programme – and particularly the last point – because of what they believe to be its reactionary implications.

Values and behaviour

With respect to values and behaviour Ynestra King writes that, 'We [i.e. women] learn early to observe, attend and nurture' (1983, p. 12) and Stephanie Leland refers to 'feminine impulses' such as 'belonging, relationship and letting be' (1983, p. 71). These are the kinds of characteristics (sometimes referred to, as

I have already remarked, as constitutive of the 'feminine principle') usually ascribed to women by ecofeminists, and, although Valerie Plumwood rightly suggests that the devaluation of male modes of thought and behaviour does not necessarily entail the affirmation of female traits, my impression is that ecofeminists usually do just that.

In support of her position Plumwood writes: 'What seems to be involved here is often not so much an affirmation of feminine connectedness with and closeness to nature as distrust and rejection of the masculine character model of disconnectedness from and domination of the natural order' (1988, p. 19). But this appears to be contradicted by, for example, Judith Plant's assertion that 'Women's values, centred around life-giving, must be revalued, elevated from their once subordinate role' (n.d., p. 7), and by Hazel Henderson's advocacy of reassessment:

> Eco-feminism . . . values motherhood and the raising and parenting of children and the maintaining of comfortable habitats and cohesive communities as the most highly productive work of society – rather than the most de-valued, as under patriarchal values and economics where the tasks are ignored and unpaid. (1983, p. 207)

It is certainly the case that male values – for example, discrimination, domination and hierarchy (Leland, 1983, pp. 68–9), and 'a disregard for the housekeeping requirements of nature' (Freer, 1983, p. 132) – are seen as positively harmful if pursued to the exclusion of other values. In this context Jean Freer scathingly characterizes the space programme as an exercise in which 'Plastic bags full of men's urine were sent to circulate endlessly in the cosmos', and then asks, 'How can they claim to be caring?' (ibid.). Ynestra King concludes:

> We see the devastation of the earth and her beings by the corporate warriors, and the threat of nuclear annihilation by the military warriors as feminist concerns. It is the same masculinist mentality which would deny us our right to our own bodies and

our own sexuality, and which depends on multiple systems of dominance and state power to have its way. (1983, p. 10)

There are several difficulties – apart from political–strategic ones – associated with the assertion of female values and the desire to upgrade them. Valerie Plumwood points out (1988, p. 21) that to begin with there is the notorious problem of identifying female traits in the first place: we could know what a representative sample of 'female' women would look like only if we already had some idea of what female traits were, but then the traits would be announced *a priori*, as it were, rather than deduced through observation. Isn't it also true to say that some men exhibit 'female' characteristics and some women 'male' characteristics, in which case such characteristics are not founded in gender as such but in, for example, socialization working on gender?

Next, there is a series of what might be considered negative traits such as subservience associated with women by women (including, of course, a large number of feminists). If we are to use woman as the yardstick for valued characteristics, we are left with no room to judge with respect to what we might suspect to be negative traits in what is regarded as typically female behaviour. We can regard subservience as negative only if we value its opposite positively, and this will mean valuing positively a characteristic normally associated with men. In other words: how are we to decide which are positive and which are negative forms of thought or behaviour? We may not want to say that all female characteristics are positive and neither do we want to argue, it seems, that all male traits are negative. But the generalized assertion that female traits are positive allows us no discriminatory purchase.

A related way of approaching this question might be to ask: given that both male and female characteristics have been developed under patriarchy, what gives us the grounds for suggesting that *either* form is worthwhile? The separatist feminist might say that what ecofeminists refer to as healthy traits are as tainted with patriarchy as unhealthy ones, and that

[195]

the only way to find out what genuine female characteristics are like (if they exist at all) would be to disengage from patriarchy as far as possible, and to let such traits 'emerge'.

Ecofeminists don't usually adopt this strategy: they simply identify some traits that they argue most women already have, they value them positively, and then suggest that both we (all of us) and therefore the planet would be better off if we adopted such traits:

> Initially it seems obvious that the ecofeminist and peace argument is grounded on accepting a special feminine connectedness with nature or with peaceful characteristics, and then asserting this as a rival ideal of the human (or as part of such an ideal). (Plumwood, 1988, p. 22)

Plumwood's own solution to the problem of identifying female traits and deciding which are positive and which are negative is strategically to sidestep the issue. She argues against the idea of accepting the feminine and rejecting the masculine (her terms) and goes instead for rejecting them both. She comes up with a 'degendered' model for the human, which

> presupposes that selection of characteristics is made on the basis of independent criteria of worth. Criteria selected will often be associated with one gender rather than another, and perhaps may turn out to resemble more closely the characteristic feminine rather than the characteristic masculine traits. But they're degendered in the sense that they won't be selected because of their connection with one gender rather than the other, but on the basis of independent considerations. (ibid., p. 23)

This project would be hard to complete (what would such 'independent considerations' look like?) and its implications cannot be followed through here. My interest in Plumwood's position is that it enables us to mark her off from what I understand to be a pair of basic ecofeminist principles: that character traits can be identified as either male or female, and that the female ones are those that most obviously need presently to be reasserted, both for our sake and for the planet's.

The subjection of women and the domination of nature

It is specific to ecofeminism that its advocates see it as good not only for women but also for the non-human natural world. Ecofeminists identify a relationship between the subjection of nature by men and the subjection of women by men. Indeed Val Plumwood defines ecofeminism as 'a body of literature whose theme is the link between the domination of women and the domination of nature' (1986, p. 120).

The nature of this link can take two forms: weak and strong. In the weak case patriarchy is seen as producing and repro-ducing its domination across a whole range of areas and anything that comes under its gaze will be subjected to it. The link between women and nature in this case is simply that they are two objects for patriarchal domination, without the subjection of one necessarily helping to produce and reproduce the subjection of the other. Thus Christine Thomas quotes Rosemary Radford Reuther: 'Women must see that there can be no liberation for them and no solution to the ecological crisis within a society whose fundamental model of relationships tends to be one of domination' (1983, p. 162).

Judith Plant makes a similar point: 'we are helping to create an awareness of domination at all levels' (n.d., p. 4), and then continues with a thought that gives a flavour of the strong link sometimes identified between women and nature in the sense of their common subjection: 'Once we understand the historical connections between women and nature and their subsequent oppression, we cannot help but take a stand on war against nature' (ibid.). This latter comment points to connections between the exploitation of women and of nature that go beyond their merely being subject to the generalized gaze of patriarchy.

Plant is suggesting that historical study of their exploitation leads to the conclusion that patriarchy has posited a particular identity between the two that produces and reproduces their common subjection. In this sense, argue the ecofeminists, the struggle for women's liberation must be a struggle for nature as well and, likewise, the despoiling of nature should not be viewed as separate from the exploitation of women. Both have their roots in patriarchy: 'We believe that a culture against nature is a culture against women' (King, 1983, p. 11).

Those who suggest a strong link argue that patriarchy confers similar characteristics on nature and on women and then systematically devalues them. Thus both are seen as irrational, uncertain, hard to control, fuzzy. Janet Biehl writes: 'In Western culture, men have traditionally justified their domination of women by conceptualising them as "closer to nature" than themselves. Women have been ideologically dehumanised and derationalised by men; called more chaotic, more mysterious in motivation, more emotional, more moist, even more polluted' (1988, p. 12). Just when this began to occur is a matter of dispute among ecofeminists. Basically the debate is between two groups – 'those who locate the problem for both women and nature in their place as part of a set of dualisms which have their origin in classical philosophy and which can be traced through a complex history to the present' and those who would rather refer to 'the rise of mechanistic science during the Enlightenment and pre-Enlightenment period' (Plumwood, 1986, p. 121). Indeed, because the first group finds no necessary relationship between the subjection of women and that of nature it is perhaps wrong to refer to them as ecofeminists.

We have already identified the ambiguous relationship that the Green movement as a whole has with Enlightenment traditions, and it is entirely consistent that some ecofeminists should see a link between the Baconian impulse to dominate nature and the subjection of women – especially once similar characteristics have been conferred on both. The modern scientific project, which has its roots in Francis Bacon, is held to be a universalizing project of reduction, fragmentation and violent control. Ecofeminists will counter this project with the feminine principles of diversity, holism, interconnectedness and non-violence. The problem with most texts that argue for these sorts of positions, though, is that they tend to paint too rosy a picture of the pre-Enlightenment period. Organicism may have given way to mechanicism, but the organicists still found reason to persecute witches. It seems that what can be said is that the mechanicist view of nature reinforced the subjection of women, but that this subjection has its roots somewhere else.

Indeed, as Janet Biehl has counterfactually suggested: 'Societies have existed that . . . could revere nature (such as ancient Egypt) and yet this "reverence" did not inhibit the development of full-blown patricentric hierarchy' (1988, p. 13). To this extent men do not need an array of thoughts justifying the subjection of nature in order to dominate women, although it seems likely that such thoughts have been used since the seventeenth century to reinforce that domination. In this way, ecofeminists who link the subjection of women and of nature cannot provide fundamental reasons for the fact of the domination of women by men, but they can point to the way in which, now, women and nature are held to possess similar characteristics and that these characteristics 'just happen' to be undervalued.

Women as 'closer to nature'

In linking the subjection of women and nature, ecofeminists point out that the intellectual structures justifying both are the same. They go on to suggest that preventing further destruction of the environment will involve being more 'in tune' with the non-human natural world, that women are habitually closer to nature than men, and that therefore women are best placed to provide role models for environmentally sensitive behaviour.

The basis of this closeness to nature is biology: 'Because of the reproductive cycle it is much harder for women to escape a sense of connection with the natural world', says Elizabeth Dodson Gray (in Plumwood, 1986, p. 125), and Hazel

[199]

Henderson remarks that, 'Biologically, most women in the world do still vividly experience their embeddedness in Nature, and can harbour few illusions concerning their freedom and separatedness from the cycles of birth and death' (1983, p. 207). Maori women bury their afterbirth in the earth as a symbolic representation of the connectedness of women as life-givers and the Earth as the source and fount of all life.

This evidently bears upon the Green movement's general aspiration to have us living more lightly on the Earth. As we saw in Chapter 2, deep ecologists argue for a change of consciousness with respect to our dealings with the non-human natural world. Warwick Fox wants a shift in priorities such that those who interfere with the environment should have to justify doing so, rather than having the onus of justification rest on the environment's defenders. A precondition for this, he argues, is an awareness of the 'soft' boundaries between ourselves and the non-human natural world. I pointed out at the time that in this connection deep ecologists are presented with a formidable problem of persuasion – most people simply do not think like that and it is hard to see how they ever will.

Ecofeminists, though, suggest that there are already millions of people thinking like that, or at least potentially on the brink of doing so – women themselves. On this reading, women's closeness to nature puts them in the Green political vanguard, in touch with a world that Judith Plant describes and that many members of the Green movement would like to see resurrected – a world in which 'rituals were carried out by miners: offerings to the gods of the soil and the subterranean world, ceremonial sacrifices, sexual abstinence and fasting were conducted and observed before violating what was considered to be the sacred earth' (n.d., p. 3).

One problem that ecofeminism needs to confront in the context of the wider aims of the Green movement is the reconciliation of the demand for positive evaluation of the activity of childbirth, and the need to reduce population levels. Of course there is no need for such an evaluation to imply a large number of actual births, but a culture that held childbirth in high esteem might find it hard to legitimize population control policies. But again, in the properly functioning sustainable society, people would learn to reach and maintain sustainable reproductive rates, much as members of a number of communities (particularly in Africa and Latin America) already do.

Questioning ecofeminism

Ecofeminism has not been without its critics and Janet Biehl, for one, believes that the linking of women with nature and the subsequent subordination of both is precisely the reason why it is dangerous to try to use the link for emancipatory purposes. Valerie Plumwood, too, makes it absolutely clear why ecofeminism is seen in some quarters of the feminist movement as reactionary: 'The concept of nature . . . has been and remains a major tool in the armoury of conservatives intent on keeping women in their place', and, 'Given this background, it is not surprising that many feminists regard with some suspicion a recent view, expressed by a growing number of writers in the ecofeminist camp, that there may be something to be said *in favour* of feminine connectedness with nature' (1988, p. 16).

Biehl's critique is principally aimed at deep ecologists, whom she sees as engaged on a project that will guarantee the domination of women by men, but her remarks are equally applicable to ecofeminism in general as I've described it. Women should not be asked, she writes, to 'think like a mountain' – in the context of women's struggle for selfhood, autonomy and acceptance as rational beings, this amounts to 'a blatant slap in the face' (ibid., p. 14). She parodies deep ecologists (and ecofeminists) who claim that 'male' values and characteristics are worthless: 'Never mind becoming rational; never mind the self; look where it got men, after all; women were better-off than men all along without that tiresome individuality' (ibid., p. 13).

The deep ecological attempt to encourage us to virtues of modesty, passivity and humility with respect to the natural world (and to other human beings), it is argued, can only

[201]

backfire in the context of women's liberation. From this point of view the women's movement has precisely been about undoing modesty and humility (and refusing to bear a child every 10 or 12 months) because these characteristics have worked in favour of patriarchy. In the context of patriarchy (i.e. now), women cannot afford to follow the deep ecological programme, and to the degree that ecofeminism subscribes to deep ecological parameters it does women no favours either: 'it is precisely humility, with its passive and receptive obedience to men, that women are trying to escape today' (ibid., p. 14).

These worries seem well founded, in that at one level ecofeminism amounts to asking people in general to adopt 'female' ways of relating to the world in the knowledge that women are more likely to do so than men. If this happens, and if such ways of relating to the world and their devaluation are indeed part of the reason for women's subordination to men, then women's position can only get worse. Ecofeminism proposes a dangerous strategy – to use ideas that have already been turned against women in the belief that, if they are taken up and lived by everyone, then a general improvement in both the human and non-human condition will result. If they are not taken up, then women will have 'sacrificed themselves to the environment', and this is a price some feminists are clearly not prepared to pay.

Concluding ecofeminism

Behind this debate lurks a point of widespread interest for the Green movement in general. Janet Biehl's (for example) desire to keep nature at arm's length appears to be founded on the privileging of rationality, autonomy and so on, and the idea that nature does not have these characteristics. Given that it doesn't have them, and given that women aspire to them, women need to dissociate themselves from nature rather than immerse themselves in it, she implies. But if this heralds good news for women, it leaves nature rather undefended: 'behind the view that there is something insulting or degrading about linking women and nature stands an unstated set of assumptions about the inferior status of the non-human world' (Plumwood, 1988, p. 18). And it is just this unstated set of assumptions, of course, that political ecologists of all types and both genders consider to be at the root of environmental degradation. It seems that the options are limited: either women side with nature and face the possibility of tightening their own subordination, or they seek liberation in terms disconnected from nature and abandon it to its fate as a resource.

This dilemma mirrors the wider debate within the feminist movement identified at the beginning of this ecofeminist section of the chapter. As I understand it, and speaking very broadly, there are presently two principal faces to feminism. The first argues for parity with men on terms substantially dictated by men. In this case women claim recognition for their rationality and autonomy (for example), and thus accept – even demand – the absorption of women into what some feminists would regard as loaded (male) definitions of humanity. These other feminists suspect that there is such a thing as liberation for women as women – not just in the sense of getting political–institutional structures to realize that women have specific problems in society, but in the sense that society itself (i.e. patriarchal society) might suppress 'womanly' ways of thinking and acting.

The problem this latter group faces is to discover just what these ways of thinking and acting are. As I understand it, separatist feminists try to answer this question by finding space outside patriarchy in order to let the 'woman' emerge. They suggest that they will never find out what liberation for women as women looks like unless they have a chance to find out what 'woman' is, and that this is impossible as long as they live alongside men.

Ecofeminists also argue for specifically female ways of thinking and acting, but claim (most of them, I think) that separatism is not necessary. As we saw earlier, ecofeminists identify a set of values and practices that women already possess to a greater degree than men, and that this justifies us in calling them female values and practices. Moreover, ecofeminists would like to see these practices 'developed and come to dominate' (Plumwood, 1988, p. 21). To this extent eco-feminists can be seen as a section of the so-called 'difference theorists' within feminism in general. They suspect that women's liberation will not be a matter of absorption into a universe whose values are male-created, but they do not subscribe to the notion of an 'unknown and yet to be discovered feminine' (ibid.). They take the differences to be what they are rather than what they might be.

Conclusion

The differences between what I have called environmentalism and ecologism are now established. Ecologism seeks radically to call into question a whole series of political, economic and social practices in a way that environmentalism does not. Ecologism envisages a post-industrial future that is quite distinct from that with which we are most generally acquainted. While most post-industrial futures revolve around high-growth, high-technology, expanding services, greater leisure, and satisfaction conceived in material terms, ecologism's post-industrial society questions growth and technology, and suggests that the Good Life will involve more work and fewer material objects. Fundamentally, ecologism takes seriously the universal condition of the finitude of the planet and asks what kinds of political, economic and social practices are (a) possible and (b) desirable within that framework. Environmentalism, typically, does no such thing.

In terms of human relationships with the non-human natural world, ecologism asks that the onus of justification be shifted from those who counsel as little interference as possible with the non-human natural world, to those who believe that interference is essentially non-problematic. Environmentalists will usually be concerned about intervention only as far as it might affect human beings; ecologists will argue that the strong anthropocentrism that this betrays is far more a part of our current problems than a solution to them.

Practical considerations of limits to growth and ethical concerns about the non-human natural world combine to produce, in ecologism, a political ideology in its own right. We

[205]

can call it an ideology (in the functional sense) because it has, first, a description of the political and social world – a pair of Green spectacles – which helps us to find our way around it. It also has a programme for political change and, crucially, it has a picture of the kind of society that ecologists think we ought to inhabit – best described as the 'sustainable society'. Because the descriptive and prescriptive elements in the political-ecological programme cannot be accommodated within other political ideologies (such as socialism) without substantially changing them, we are surely entitled to set ecologism alongside such ideologies, competing with them in the late-twentieth-century political marketplace. In contrast, I maintain that the various sorts of environmentalism (conservation, pollution control, waste recycling, etc.) can be slotted with relative ease into more well-known ideological paradigms, and that the current vogue for green (small 'g') politics shows this co-option at work.

But what of the relationship between ecologism and environmentalism? One obvious way into this is to see ecologism as the Utopian picture that all political movements need if they are to operate effectively. On this reading, Green politics has a reformist as well as a radical wing, with the latter acting as a kind of puritan policeman, calling the reformists to order when they stray too far off line during their 'march through the institutions'. This is as much as to say that questions about whether or not the dark-Green picture as I have described it in this book is realizable are to miss the point. Indeed, its Utopianism, with the vision, hard work and committed creativity that it can generate, is, on this reading, ecologism's strongest card.

More positively still, the Utopian vision provides the indispensable fundamentalist well of inspiration from which green activists, even the most reformist and respectable, need continually to draw. Green reformers need a radically alternative picture of post-industrial society, they need deep ecological visionaries, they need the phantom studies of the sustainable society, and they need, paradoxically, occasionally to be brought down to earth and to be reminded about limits to growth. Dark-Green politics reminds us of where we want to go even if we don't really think we can get there. On this view, there is what we might call a 'constructive tension' between ecologism and environmentalism. But is it so obvious that the tension is constructive?

Towards the end of 1988 Jonathon Porritt, the leading spokesperson for Green politics in Britain and an increasingly influential figure on the international scene, appeared on BBC television's weekly topical current affairs programme *Question Time*. It was not his first appearance on the programme, but on this occasion he was unusually the centre of attention throughout, benefiting from the general surge of interest in environmental issues that took place throughout that year, and the particular filip given to the subject by Prime Minister Margaret Thatcher's environmental 'conversion' at the end of September.

In the fifty-ninth minute of the hour-long programme something interesting happened: Porritt mentioned that there was a difference between light-green and dark-Green politics. The programme's presenter, Sir Robin Day, asked him to explain the difference and Porrit didn't manage to do so – not surprisingly, given the short time left to him. The fact that the subject did not crop up until the programme had effectively finished, and the further fact that the question was not answered, are both symptomatic of the present state of Green politics, at least in Britain. That is: Green politics as such is virtually invisible.

Ironically, this could be significantly the result of the recent explosion in the political popularity of environmental issues. It might seem curious to suggest that Green politics is currently the victim of its own (partial) success but, from a point of view that has it that the tension between environmentalism and ecologism is destructive rather than constructive, that may be what has happened. The Green movement has spent years trying to get the environment onto the political agenda, and now that this has been accomplished it seems unsure where to go next. What is clear is that if it stays where it presently and publicly is – a watchdog for newly 'greened' major political parties – it may be in danger of disappearing behind brighter lights and louder voices, or even of undermining what I understand to be its *raison d'être*: the call for radical social, political and economic change.

There was a significant moment in this context at the British Green Party's National Conference in October 1988. The first full day of the conference coincided with the last day of the Conservative Party Conference in Brighton. Only a few days earlier Margaret Thatcher had made her famous 'conversion' speech to the Royal Society and rumour had it that she would seek to drive home her environmental message in Brighton. With this in mind, and in the hope of obtaining some interesting footage, the television companies following the Green Party Conference invited leading members of the party to be filmed and recorded watching, and commenting upon, the Prime Minister's televised speech. They agreed, and we were treated to the most curious of events – Margaret Thatcher apparently making peace with the environment while those who have spent ten or more years trying to get her to do just that sat, in a silence only occasionally punctuated by the juicy ripostes the television crews were hoping for, wondering (it seemed to me) what to do next.

Of course those leading members of the Green Party know perfectly well how to respond to environmental speeches such as the one Margaret Thatcher made that day. They know that there is more, much more, to Green politics than talking about planetary stewardship, but they are not at all used to letting us know how much more. Returning for a moment to Robin Day's *Question Time*, Jonathon Porritt had spoken for much of the evening as a light-green Green, as he is wont to do in that kind of company and in front of that kind of audience. In this he is no different from the majority of Greens, who turn green in certain public forums either because they think that to be Green would be to marginalize themselves, or because the discussions in those forums (particularly in television and radio) are weighted towards what already interests the public (polluted rivers, dying seals) rather than what might interest them if they got the chance to hear about it. Either way, one effect of these silences has been to make the noise of Green politics inaudible to all but the most involved.

Porritt and those who think like him are evidently in an uncomfortable position. On the one hand they have a message to give, and on the other hand they are confronted by a public and culture that they think prevents them from giving it. There is nothing new in this: it is the typical dilemma of any radical form of politics, and it can produce a burdensome form of political schizophrenia. In this context, Porritt himself has described how being both director of Friends of the Earth and an individual member of the Green Party (Dodds, 1988, p. 201) has pulled him in different directions at the same time.

It works like this: there is a desire to popularize Green politics, to 'get the message across', and there is a desire to make sure that the message is indeed Green and not merely green. But the rub appears to be that, in order to get any message across at all, it has to be green and not Green. Porritt refers, for example, to FoE's highly successful campaign to encourage producers to phase out the use of chlorofluorocarbons in aerosols. He notes that by the end of 1989 only some 5 or 10 per cent of aerosols will use CFCs, compared with nearly three-quarters just a year or so earlier. This, as he writes, is 'All good stuff – a small, incremental step towards a safer environment'. Then he asks: 'But does it actually bring us anywhere nearer sustainability?' (ibid., pp. 200–1). And of course this is the point – eradicating CFCs from aerosols is a green achievement, but is it a Green one?

Some have suspected that it is not. As Porritt himself observes:

Various deep Greens (including members of the Green Party) were quick to castigate Friends of the Earth for not campaigning against aerosols in general, inasmuch as they are indisputably unnecessary, wasteful and far from environmentally benign even if they don't use CFCs. Such critics suggested (and who can blame them?) that by campaigning *for* CFC-free aerosols, we were in fact condoning, if not positively promoting, self-indulgence, vanity, and wholly unsustainable patterns of consumption. (ibid., p. 201)

This catches the dilemma in all its radicality: if, as the final phrases suggest, environmental campaigns can contribute to unsustainability, then light-green and dark-Green politics are in conflict rather than in concert – the notion of 'constructive tension' is called into question. In other words, it is not simply a semantic question about whether or not Green and green mean the same thing and, if not, how different they are, but a question that has political–strategic implications. If Green and green pull in different directions, then this is serious indeed, because the classic defence of the political schizophrenic is that, even if the two positions are in different places, at least they are on the same track. Put differently, the light-green Jonathon Porritt will argue that light-green education can lead to dark-Green radicalization; that the normal course of things is for the former to evolve into the latter: 'On balance I believe that more good will be done than harm *if* one sees such an approach as part of a transitional strategy' (ibid., p. 199).

He might even begrudgingly suggest that anything is better than nothing, even if no evolution takes place at all: 'After all, confronted with the choice between green yuppies or naturally nasty yuppies, between mindful green consumers or relatively mindless, old-style consumers, it's your proverbial Hobson's choice' (ibid.). In these senses Porritt can happily defend his environmentalist postures on *Question Time* because his highly effective interventions might green the odd yuppy and improve the Body Shop's annual turnover. But what will Porritt the ecologist think of all this? Is his popularity as an environmentalist bought at the cost of his more radical, mostly private convictions? This is the kind of question he might have had to answer on *Question Time* if Green politics really was on the political agenda.

A central strategic issue to be confronted by the Green

movement, then, is: does light-green politics (environmental-ism) make dark-Green politics (ecologism) more or less likely? Roughly speaking, it will be held to be more likely if it is believed that both forms of politics are heading in the same direction, even though one might lag slightly behind the other. It will be held to be less likely, if it is believed that these forms of politics work more substantially against rather than with each other. In this latter case the conclusion will not be to encourage people to see environmentalism as a 'transitional strategy' for ecologism, but to argue that it is no transitional strategy at all.

There are, of course, arguments for and against both positions. Raising environmental awareness, for example, may well seem to be the key to more radical change in that it sensitizes us to the dangers of present social and economic practices. It provides us with a green platform, a new consensus on our relationship with our environment, from which we can make the leap to more radically Green practices. But it may, on the other hand, constitute a barrier rather than a platform. It may, from a dark-Green point of view, immunize rather than sensitize, by obscuring the informing principle of Green politics: that infinite growth in a finite system is impossible, and that therefore green production and consumption are (in the long term) as unsustainable as present forms of production and consumption. On this reading, environmentalism saps radical energy and pulls up the drawbridge against Green change.

If some people in the Green movement itself seem to have opted for the first position, then that may be because of an unwillingness to disturb the relatively calm (surface) waters of Green politics. Porritt and Winner, for example, refer to the strategic gaps between light and dark Greens in Britain as 'disagreements that can and should lead to constructive convergence rather than negative divergence. Greens must guard against these disagreements becoming sterile or violent internal feuds of the kind that have plagued the political left for most of the last eighty years' (1988, p. 260).

Perhaps they should, but perhaps, too, environmentalism and ecologism just are negatively divergent. Indeed Porritt

[211]

himself, for one, appears unsure (in other moments) which line to take. We have seen him 'on balance', above, arguing in favour of the 'transitional strategy' notion, but he is equally aware of the traps it lays, especially in its green consumerist disguise:

> At best, it may mitigate the most immediate symptoms of ecological decline, but the short-term advantages gained in the process are almost certainly outweighed by the simultaneous immunisation of such consumers against reality . . . Green consumerism may marginally assist environmentalists in some of their campaigns, but its very effectiveness depends on not attempting to do down or supplant today's industrial order, and on not promoting awareness of its inherent unsustainability. (In Dodds, 1988, pp. 199–200)

And so we find ourselves back at square one: the radical Green demand to call today's industrial order into question. But how to do it? Friends of the Earth was faced with the fact in its CFC campaign that it 'would have made little, if any, headway with an anti-aerosol campaign' (ibid., p. 201), even though calling today's industrial order into question would have involved just that. Jonathon Porritt wants at least as much 'to be out there explaining why the old mechanistic world view of Bacon, Descartes and Newton is now wholly redundant . . . as to be arguing the merits of flue gas desulphurisation' (ibid., p. 203). The dangers of him doing so are apparent: Green politics might just disappear without trace. But by the same token we cannot properly gauge the future of Green politics unless he, and others like him, give it a go. Towards the end of 1988 various environmental groups got together to throw down the 'Green Gauntlet' before the government – a list of areas for environmental action, constituting a test of the government's environmental good faith. This will certainly help keep the government on its toes, but perhaps the time is ripe for Greens to pick up their own gauntlet. 'If the movement is to grow to the point where it will suppress the "outdated" ideologies of capitalism and socialism . . . it will, it is a fair bet, have to mobilise this

[212]

"dark-Green" side as well as the "light-Green" forces of reasoning, debating and campaigning', wrote John Lloyd (not a member of the Green movement) in the *Sunday Times* magazine of 26 February 1989. This is as if to say that Act One of the Green movement's paradise play is over, and it is time that the curtain was lifted on Act Two.

Bibliography

Allaby, M. and Bunyard, P. (1980), *The Politics of Self-Sufficiency* (Oxford: Oxford University Press)

Anderson, F. R. *et al.* (n.d.), *Environmental Protection: Law and Policy* (Little, Brown and Co.)

Attfield, R. (1983), *The Ethics of Environmental Concern* (Oxford: Blackwell)

Bahro, R. (1982), *Socialism and Survival* (London: Heretic Books)

Bahro, R. (1986), *Building the Green Movement* (London: GMP)

Bauman, Z. (1987), *Legislators and Interpreters* (Oxford: Polity)

Biehl, J. (1988), in *Green Line*, 59, February

Bookchin, M. (1972), *Post-Scarcity Anarchism* (Montreal: Black Rose Books)

Bookchin, M. (1982), *The Ecology of Freedom* (Palo Alto: Cheshire Books)

Bookchin, M. (1986), *The Modern Crisis* (Philadelphia: New Society)

Bottomore, T. (1982), *Elites and Society* (Harmondsworth: Penguin)

Bottomore, T. and Rubel, M. (1984), *Karl Marx: Selected Writings in Sociology and Social Philosophy* (Harmondsworth: Penguin)

Bramwell, A. (1989), *Ecology in the 20th Century* (New Haven and London: Yale University Press)

Brennan, A. (1988), *Thinking about Nature* (London: Routledge)

British Ecology Party Manifesto (1983) (London: Ecology Party)

British Green Party Manifesto (1987) (London: Green Party)

Brundtland, Gro Harlem (1989), 'Economía ecológica', *El País* (Temas de nuestra época), 30 March, p. 4

Brundtland Report (n.d.), *Our common future* (London: Earthscan)

Bunyard, P. and Morgan–Grenville, F. (eds) (1987), *The Green Alternative* (London: Methuen)

Caldecott, L. and Leland, S. (1983), *Reclaim the Earth* (London: Women's Press)

Capra, F. (1985), *The Turning Point* (London: Flamingo)

Clark, S. (1983), 'Gaia and the forms of life' in Elliot and Gare (1983)

Collard, A. and Contrucci, J. (1988), *Rape of the Wild* (London: The Women's Press)

[214]

Conford, P. (1988), *The Organic Tradition* (Bideford: Green Books)
Conroy, C. and Litvinoff, P. (eds) (1988), *The Greening of Aid* (London: Earthscan)

Daly, H. (ed.) (197?), *Toward a Steady-State Economy* (San Francisco: Freeman)
Daly, H. (1977a), 'The politics of the sustainable society', in Pirages (1977a)
Daly, H. (1977b), 'The steady-state economy: what, why, and how', in Pirages (1977a)
Dauncey, G. (1988), *After the Crash* (Basingstoke: Green Print)
Devall, B. (1980), 'The Deep Ecology movement', Natural Resources Journal, vol. 20
Dobson, A. (1989), 'Deep ecology', *Cogito*
Dodds, F. (ed.) (1988), *Into the 21st Century* (Basingstoke: Green Print).
Donald, J. and Hall, S. (1986), *Politics and Ideology* (Milton Keynes: Open University Press)

Eckersley, R. (1987), 'Green politics: A practice in search of a theory', paper delivered at the Ecopolitics II Conference, University of Tasmania, 22–25 May 1987
Ekins, P. (ed.) (1986), *The Living Economy* (London: Routledge & Kegan Paul)
Elkington, J. and Burke, T. (1987), *The Green Capitalists* (London: Victor Gollancz)
Elliot, R. and Gare, A. (eds) (1983), *Environmental Philosophy* (Milton Keynes: Open University Press)

Feuer, L. (1976), *Marx and Engels: Basic Writings on Politics and Philosophy* (Glasgow: Fontana)
Fox, W. (1984), 'Deep ecology: a new philosophy of our time?', *The Ecologist*, vol. 14, no. 5/6
Fox, W. (1986a), *Approaching Deep Ecology: A Response to Richard Sylvan's Critique of Deep Ecology* (Tasmania: University of Tasmania)
Fox, W. (1986b), 'Ways of thinking environmentally', talk given to 4th National Environmental Education Conference, Australia, September
Frankel, B. (1987), *The Post-Industrial Utopians* (Oxford: Polity Press)
Frankland, E. G. (1988), 'The role of the Greens in West German parliamentary politics, 1980–87', *The Review of Politics*, Winter
Freer, J. (1983), 'Gaea: the Earth as our spiritual heritage', in Caldecott and Leland (1983)

German Green Party Manifesto (1983) (London: Heretic Books)
Goldsmith, E. (1972), *A Blueprint for Survival* (London: Tom Stacey)
Goldsmith, E. and Hildyard, N. (1986), *Green Britain or Industrial Wasteland?* (Oxford: Polity Press)

[215]

Goldsmith, E. (1988), *The Great U-Turn: De-Industrializing Society* (Bideford: Green Books)

Goodwin, B. (1987), *Using Political Ideas* (Chichester: John Wiley)

Gorz, A. (1982), *Farewell to the Working-Class* (London: Pluto)

Gorz, A. (1985), *Paths to Paradise/On the Liberation from Work* (London: Pluto)

Gould, P. (1988), *Early Green Politics* (Brighton: Harvester Press)

Hampson, N. (1979), *The Enlightenment* (Harmondsworth: Penguin)

Harper, P. (n.d.), 'Life at the Quarry' (unpublished)

Heilbroner, R. (1974), *An Inquiry into the Human Prospect* (New York: Harper and Row)

Henderson, H. (1983), 'The warp and the weft: the coming synthesis of eco-philosophy and eco-feminism', in Caldecott and Leland (1983)

Hülsberg, W. (1988), *The German Greens* (London and New York: Verso)

Irvine, S. and Ponton, A. (1988), *A Green Manifesto: Policies for a Green Future* (London: Macdonald Optima)

Irvine, S. (1989), *Beyond Green Consumerism* (London: Friends of the Earth)

King, Y. (1983), 'The eco-feminist imperative', in Caldecott and Leland (1983)

Kumar, S. (ed.) (1984), *The Schumacher Lectures: Volume II* (London: Blond & Briggs)

Lee, K. (1989), *Social Philosophy and Ecological Scarcity* (London: Routledge)

Leland, S. (1983), 'Feminism and ecology: theoretical connections', in Caldecott and Leland (1983)

Leopold, A. (1949), *A Sand County Almanac* (Oxford: Oxford University Press)

Lovelock, J. (1979, *Gaia* (Oxford: Oxford University Press)

Lovelock, J. (1986), 'Gaia: the world as living organism', *New Scientist*, 18 December

McLellan, D. (1986), *Ideology* (Milton Keynes: Open University Press)

Marien, M. (1977), 'The two visions of post-industrial society', *Futures*, October

Meadows, D. H., Meadows, D. L., Randers, J., and Behrens III, W. (1983), *The Limits to Growth* (London: Pan)

Midgley, M. (1983a), *Animals and Why They Matter* (Harmondsworth: Penguin)

Midgley, M. (1983b), 'Duties concerning islands', in Elliot and Gare (1983)

Myers, N. (1985), *The Gaia Atlas of Planet Management* (London: Good Books)

Naess, A. (1973), 'The shallow and the deep, long-range ecology movement. A summary', *Inquiry*, 16
Naess, A. (1984), 'Intuition, intrinsic value and deep ecology', *The Ecologist*, vol. 14, no. 5/6
Naess, A. (1989), *Ecology, Community and Lifestyle* (Cambridge: Cambridge University Press)

Ophuls, W. (1977), 'The politics of a sustainable society', in Pirages (1977a)
O'Riordan, T. (1981), *Environmentalism* (London: Pion)

Pepper, D. (1984), *The Roots of Modern Environmentalism* (Beckenham: Croom Helm)
Pirages, D. (ed.) (1977a), *The Sustainable Society* (New York: Praeger)
Pirages, D. (1977b), 'Introduction: a social design for sustainable growth', in Pirages (1977a)
Plant, J. (n.d.), 'Women and nature', *Green Line*, offprint
Plumwood, V. (1986), 'Ecofeminism: an overview and discussion of positions and arguments', in *Women and Philosophy*, supplement to the *Australasian Journal of Philosophy*, vol. 64, June
Plumwood, V. (1988), 'Women, humanity and nature', *Radical Philosophy*, Spring
Porritt, J. (1984), interview in *Marxism Today*, March
Porritt, J. (1986), *Seeing Green* (Oxford: Blackwell)
Porritt, J. and Winner, D. (1988), *The Coming of the Greens* (London: Fontana)

Redclift, M. (1987), *Sustainable Development* (London: Methuen)
Reed, C. (1988), 'Wild men of the woods', *Guardian*, 13 July
Regan, T. (1988), *The Case for Animal Rights* (London: Routledge)
Richards, F. (1989), 'Can capitalism go Green?', *Living Marxism*, 4, February
Roderick, R. (1986), *Habermas and the Foundations of Critical Theory* (London: Macmillan)
Rolston, H. (1983), 'Are values in nature subjective or objective', in Elliot and Gare (1983)
Ryle, M. (1988), *Ecology and Socialism* (London: Rodins)

Sale, K. (1984), 'Mother of all: an introduction to bioregionalism', in Kumar (1984)

Sale, K. (1985), *Dwellers in the Land: the Bioregional Vision* (San Francisco: Sierra Club)

Sallen, A. K. (1984), 'Deeper than Deep Ecology: the eco-feminist connection', *Environmental Ethics*, vol. 6

Schumacher, E. (1976), *Small is Beautiful* (London: Sphere)

Schwarz, W. and Schwarz, D. (1987), *Breaking Through* (Bideford: Green Books)

Seabrook, J. (1988), *The Race for Riches* (Basingstoke: Green Print)

Seymour, J. and Girardet, H. (1987), *Blueprint for a Green Planet* (London: Dorling Kindersley)

Shiva, V. (1988), *Staying Alive* (London: Zed Books)

Simonon, L. (1983), 'Personal, political and planetary play', in Caldecott and Leland (1983)

Spretnak, C. and Capra, F. (1985), *Green Politics* (London: Paladin)

Strong, D. M. (1988), *Dreamers and Defenders: American Conservationists* (Lincoln and London: University of Nebraska Press)

Sylvan, R. (1984a), 'A critique of deep ecology' (part one), *Radical Philosophy*, 40; (1984b) (part two), *Radical Philosophy*, 41

Thomas, C. (1983), 'Alternative technology: a feminist technology?', in Caldecott and Leland (1983)

Thompson, J. (1983), 'Preservation of wilderness and the Good Life', in Elliot and Gare (1983)

Tokar, B. (1987), *The Green Alternative* (San Pedro: R. and E. Miles)

Tokar, B. (1988), 'Social ecology, deep ecology and the future of Green thought', *The Ecologist*, vol. 18, no. 4/5

Ward, B. and Dubos, R. (1972), *Only One Earth: The Care and Maintenance of a Small Planet* (London: André Deutsch)

Warren, K. J. (1987), 'Feminism and ecology: making connections', *Environmental Ethics*, vol. 9

Weston, J. (ed.) (1986), *Red and Green* (London: Pluto)

Williams, R. (n.d.), *Socialism and Ecology* (London: SERA)

Williams, R. (1986), *Towards 2000* (Harmondsworth: Pelican)

Index